——————— MIND MATTERS ———————

Art or Bunk?

————— MIND MATTERS —————

series editor: Judith Hughes

——————— MIND MATTERS ———————

art or bunk?

IAN GROUND

PUBLISHED BY BRISTOL CLASSICAL PRESS

First published 1989 by Bristol Classical Press

Bristol Classical Press
is an imprint of
Gerald Duckworth & Co. Ltd
The Old Piano Factory
48 Hoxton Square, London N1 6PB

Reprinted 1993

A catalogue record for this book is available
from the British Library

ISBN 1-85399-015-9

Printed in Great Britain by
The Cromwell Press Ltd, Melksham, Wiltshire

for Jenny

contents

foreword

'A philosophical problem has the form *I don't know my way about*,' said Wittgenstein. These problems are not the ones where we need information, but those where we are lost for lack of adequate signposts and landmarks. Finding our way – making sense out of the current confusions and becoming able to map things both for ourselves and for others – is doing successful philosophy. This is not quite what the lady meant who told me when I was seven that I ought to have more philosophy, because philosophy was eating up your cabbage and not making a fuss about it. But that lady *was* right to suggest that there were some useful skills here.

Philosophizing, then, is not just a form of highbrow chess for postgraduate students; it is becoming conscious of the shape of our lives, and anybody may need to do it. Our culture contains an ancient tradition which is rich in helpful ways of doing so, and in Europe they study that tradition at school. Here, that study is at present being squeezed out even from university courses. But that cannot stop us doing it if we want to. This series contains excellent guide-books for people who do want to, guide-books which are clear, but which are not superficial surveys. They are themselves pieces of real philosophy, directed at specific problems which are likely to concern all of us. Read them.

MARY MIDGLEY

preface

Philosophers are very good at talking to one another. Some of them are also good at talking with other people. In the market-places of Athens, the cafés of Paris, and lately, in the pubs of London, philosophers have always found a public bursting with its own ideas and keen to discuss them with others. The need to ask and attempt to answer philosophical questions is in us all and is prompted sometimes by particular events in our personal lives and sometimes by a more general unease about wider social or political or scientific issues. At such times there is always a popular demand for philosophers to explain themselves and the views of their illustrious forebears in ways which others can understand and question and use.

It is not an easy thing to do because Philosophy is not easy, though its central insights, like those in the sciences, are often startingly simple. To gain those insights we all have to follow the paths of reasoning for ourselves. Signposts have been left for us by the great philosophers of the past, and deciphering some of them is part of the business of this series.

'Mind Matters' is not 'Philosophy Made Easy' but rather 'Philosophy Made Intelligible', and the authors in this series have been chosen for more than their philosophical knowledge. Some of them are also experts in other fields such as medicine, computing or biology. All are people who recognise and try to practise the art of writing in an accessible and clear manner, believing that philosophical thought which is not under-standable is best kept to oneself. Many have acquired this ability in the harsh discipline of adult education where students bring their own knowledge and puzzles to the subject and demand real explanations of relevant issues.

Each book in this series begins with a perplexing question that we may ask ourselves without, perhaps, realising that we are 'philosophising': Do computers have minds? Can a pile of bricks be a work of art? Should we hold pathological killers responsible for their crimes? Such questions are considered and new questions raised with frequent reference to the views of major philosophers. The authors go further than this, however. It is not their intention to produce a potted history of philosophical ideas. They also make their own contributions to the subject, suggesting different avenues of thought to explore. The result is a collection of original writings on a wide range of topics produced for all those who find Philosophy as fascinating and compelling as they do.

For many people, the infamous pile of bricks in the Tate Gallery, Carl Andre's *Equivalent VIII*, is still the most potent symbol of modern art, and it is what inspires Ian Ground's question 'Art or Bunk?'

Using his wide knowledge of classical aesthetics and current ideas in the philosophy of art, he guides us through various attempts to say just what sort of thing a work of art is, and shows us a way to answer the question.

Although his examples relate to the visual arts, his arguments are applicable to arts in general, and his book provides a much-needed, lively and readable introduction to aesthetics.

JUDITH HUGHES

Plate 1: Carl Andre, Equivalent VIII, © DACS, 1989.

Plate 2: Michelangelo, La Pietà. (Photo: the Mansell Collection)

1: art or bunk?

In 1972 the Tate Gallery in London purchased a work of art by the American artist, Carl Andre. It was entitled *Equivalent VIII*, and consisted of a set of 120 completely unworked fire-bricks arranged in a rectangle (see Plate 1). The furore and public passion the subsequent 'Bricks Affair' excited were extraordinary. In fact, *Equivalent VIII* accidentally succeeded in awakening a new generation of people to an old question. Just what sort of thing is a work of art?

Why on earth this question should matter and how to go about answering it is the business of this book.

What was it about *Equivalent VIII* that was so outrageous? What could outrage even a public that was used to the idea of being outraged by artists?

a cognitive barn-dance

First of all, *Equivalent VIII* was certainly not outrageous because it was a work of art that affronted public morals, at least not in any obvious way. Even the most pretentious of art catalogue writers would have difficulty describing *Equivalent VIII* as pornographic or blasphemous or liable to corrupt the young.

Secondly, it was not simply that the taxpayers, or for that matter anybody, had paid some £4,000 for a work of art. Though the art market in 1972 was not subject to quite the same inflationary pressures prevalent today, the public was quite used to the idea of works of art fetching relatively large sums of money. It may have been that financial considerations were part of the public outrage, but what really lay at the bottom

1

of it was something quite different and quite unusual.

In fact *Equivalent VIII* did not outrage the public because, as a work of art, it meant anything or did anything or had been bought at some particular price. Rather, what the public at large found so outrageous was simply *the fact that Equivalent VIII could be considered to be a work of art at all.*

It is important to understand what was at stake here. Again let us proceed by seeing what the public mind was not concerned with.

It was not that anybody thought that Andre's bricks in some way or other fell short of being a work of art in the way that, for example, I might fall just short of qualifying for a sports team because I am just not quite fast enough a runner. There are two reasons why this wasn't so. In the first place, we are, if we think about it, quite familiar with the idea that artists produce things which, one way or another, have fallen short of being works of art. We call them roughs or preparatory works. And, of course, sometimes people buy such things and value them more than they ought. Like other sorts of object which are not works of art, sometimes such things do end up in galleries and museums alongside works of art. We will return to consider some ways in which this can happen in the next chapter. But Andre's bricks were not outrageous because they were obviously a first attempt idiotically mistaken for the finished article.

Secondly, and more important, it was clear to many people that there was simply no way in which Andre's bricks *could* just fail to be a work of art. The problem was more serious than that. It was not that the work only just failed. The problem was that *Equivalent VIII* was nowhere near succeeding.

But again this was not because Andre's bricks failed so miserably in being a work of art that they were hardly worth calling even a failed attempt; that calling the arrangement of bricks a failed work of art gave it credit it didn't deserve. In this way, for example, I might be a seriously incompetent tennis player – never able to serve the ball, always missing returns, a bit hazy about the rules and so on. And I might be so bad that someone who would justifiably hesitate to describe me as a tennis player, might also hesitate to describe me as a bad tennis player. But this was not the thought. It was not that anyone could think that Andre knew what he was doing when really he completely lacked any such competence.

The problem was this. People could not understand how Andre had managed to fail in making a work of art at all. They knew that what he had produced was not a work of art in the same way that a glass of water or someone's auntie or a pile of old newspapers lying in a cupboard are not works of art. Such things are not works of art in the sort of way that animals are not astronomical events and cauliflowers are not kings. They belong to entirely different categories.

We all know, if we bother to think of it, that we cannot in the normal run of things even *try* to point at a cauliflower but point at a king by mistake. It was felt, then, by those who thought that Andre had not made a work of art, that he had not done so only in the way that I don't make a work of art when I eat my breakfast. That is, in a way that has nothing whatsoever to do with trying to make works of art. He was not in error or in need of a little, or even a lot more, practice. Not at all. He was cognitively barn-dancing. For no one could try to make a work of art by doing what he had done.

bunk

Consequently, for those who held this view, anyone who believes Andre's implicit claim even to have been trying to make a work of art thereby shows that he does not understand the difference between a work of art and anything else. Between, they might say, that rare, special, unique sort of thing that is a work of art and the crassest piece of humbug, claptrap and sophistry. Between art, they might say, and what is just rubbish, nonsense, idiocy. In short, people were thinking this: 'To believe that a pile of bricks could be a work of art is not to know the difference between art and bunk.'

And indeed the thought that Andre's work was just 'bunk', seems best to capture what many people appeared to have thought and felt about it. It captures the sort of outrage that people felt in being asked to take Andre's work seriously. It is just because of this, just because of the crudity of this term, because of all that we want to say when we use it, that this term has its part in our inquiry.

So here we are close to the source of the outrage. It was not that there were supposed art 'experts', as apparently those at the Tate, who believed that Andre's work was art. The problem lies in the prior thought – that there should be any doubt at all that this was not a work of art.

This is because once aired, or admitted, a doubt of this kind throws everything into confusion. To say that such a pile of bricks might be a work of art, even that we should perhaps open our minds to such a possibility, is as if to consider the possibility that bread might not continue to nourish us or that we might now all be dreaming. Without the doubt everything is clear. But with the doubt nothing is clear any more. It was felt, then, that if it is even to be a question whether or not those unworked fire-bricks could be a work of art then no one, anywhere, knows what is meant by a 'work of art' any more.

And here, precisely, was the source of the outrage. For one reason or another, it was Andre's *Equivalent VIII* that woke the mass of people up to two facts. First, that the idea of what a work of art is supposed to be had been transformed literally out of all recognition. And second, that this transformation had been in place for many years and was now firmly consolidated. So much so, indeed, that it was now the public idea of a work of art that was thought to be the pretender and charlatan. Without the general public really noticing, mad revolutionaries, who it was always assumed someone was keeping at bay, had become elder statesmen. *Equivalent VIII* was part of Andre's internationally acknowledged corpus of work which was itself part of a recognised movement. Nothing now corresponded to what had been the idea of a work of art. Like a jewel thief's calling card, *Equivalent VIII* was a brazen message that the public had been robbed, not of money, but of what they thought they meant when they thought or spoke about works of art.

So what exactly was it about *Equivalent VIII* that made people think this way? It is this that was and remains so difficult to pin down. What one might do is to gesture towards some of its properties whilst thinking of something which no one doubts is a work of art, say Michelangelo's *Pietà* (see Plate 2). Thus one might point towards the nature of the materials used – industrial fire-bricks. Or the fact that even these were not the materials originally exhibited by Andre in New York in 1966 but only some similar bricks arranged in the same way. Or the fact that the object is visually flat, undifferentiated. Or the way that the object is presented to us – lying on the floor rather than being given some special position. Its obvious, vocal, non-uniqueness.

One might go on listing such properties. But what quickly becomes apparent is that drawing up such a list really does cut both ways. On the one hand the more items we add to the list, the more pointless an exercise it seems. We feel as if we might as well be comparing the *Pietà* with a towerblock or the top of someone's office desk. There seems to be no point in generating such contrasts.

why not fire-bricks?
On the other hand the more we reflect on such contrasts, the more intriguing they become. For example, consider more carefully the complaint that the work bought by the Tate was not even the same physical object originally exhibited by Andre, but one composed of numerically different bricks.

We might complain that the only defence of this is that the original fire-bricks were not important. But if the original bricks were not important why should the new ones be? If it does not matter that *Equivalent VIII* is composed of these particular bricks, why was the Tate so concerned when ink was spilled on them? Why bother to clean them? Why not just go out and get some more bricks? And isn't the whole thing shown to be absurd when we realise that the Tate must have those bricks insured? Yet, if the Tate were to burn down, the fire-bricks would probably be the only things to survive! I could even arrange my own bricks and have my own personal *Equivalent VIII*. But there can only be one *Pietà*. What greater contrast could there be between these two objects?

But now reflect. Just what is it that is supposed to be unique about Michelangelo's work of art? For surely it is unique. But the stuff it is made of is not unique. So it cannot be the material, the stone alone, that is special. Then it must indeed be what is done with the material and not the material itself. But something, even if not very much, has been done with the fire-bricks. They have, after all, been arranged in a certain way. But couldn't anyone arrange some bricks like that? So something special must be done with the materials. They must in some way be transformed by the artist. But then how and how much do the physical materials of which a work of art in the visual arts is made, have to be transformed, worked by the artist, to count as a work of art?

In any case, if it is how the material is worked by an artist that is crucial, then why shouldn't he use fire-bricks? What is so compulsory about granite, or bronze or wood? Aren't these in some sense 'ordinary', 'industrial' materials too? Further, why treat as absurd the idea of having one's own personal *Equivalent VIII*? Isn't an exact copy of the *Pietà* just as good as the original? If it looks the same, if it has the same appearance, then surely that is all that matters. Isn't the insistence that pieces of sculpture must be unique physical objects just a by-product of the fact that people want to own works of art and to make money by trading in them? Aren't we being misled by something that is peculiar to the visual arts and not to 'Art' with a capital 'A'? After all, my copy of *Crime and Punishment* is far from unique, yet when I read it I read a novel that is surely a work of art too. Something similar is true of music. But then why is it just obvious that *Equivalent VIII* could not be a work of art? For, despite everything, it's clear that it couldn't be.

And so on. In this way it can come to seem to us that if *Equivalent VIII* might be a work of art, then it is no longer clear what a work of art is. We may be no longer at home with our notion of art. It may seem to us that it is no longer clear what a work of art has ever been. The question of whether or not a pile of bricks can be a work of art, just in being asked, inevitably invites the question: what is a work of art?

Equivalent VIII outraged the public, then, because it raised in a peculiarly dramatic form a question to which the public had no answer. And, worse than that, it was not a new question but a very old question. A question to which it had always been assumed that we did, somewhere, have the answer, but which in fact we all find extremely problematic. Worst of all, it was a question which we did not even know how to go about answering. And, of course, by and large, that sort of a question is almost always a philosophical question.

Such philosophical questions are no ordinary sort of question. For they cannot be answered by ordinary means. In trying to answer this question, we cannot simply look up 'art' in the dictionary and hope to be enlightened. But nor can we simply look at works of art and hope to see the difference. For whose works shall we look at? Michelangelo's or Andre's?

'the aesthetic'
In fact, to answer this question demands that we undertake a philosophical inquiry into the family of concepts of which that of art is only one and by no means the most important member. As we shall see, the head of this family is the concept of the aesthetic. And we shall soon turn to examine this notion. In doing so we shall see something of why any of us should be at all concerned about our question; why it should matter that we understand what sort of a difference there is between art and bunk.

But first we should be aware that there are other members of this family of concepts. Close to the head of this family are the notions of aesthetic understanding, aesthetic interest and aesthetic knowledge. Related to these are ideas of what 'fits' and what is 'appropriate'. And also important are notions of aesthetic intention, of artistic tradition, the idea of a medium, and so on.

Indeed, this is such a large family of concepts, related in such a multitude of complex ways, that in an inquiry of this kind it is useful to provide ourselves with a kind of genealogy or map. Fig. 1 shows the notion of a work of art at the centre of a triangular network of relations. The three points of this triangle provide us with a mnemonic for three sorts of answer to our question – answers which form the fabric of the philosophical

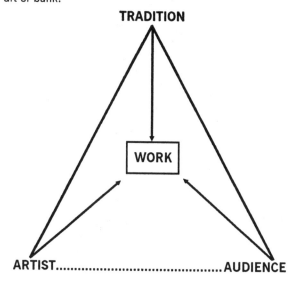

Figure 1

discussion of art and its value. Because of their importance they provide the structure of our discussion.

A. **Art and the artist.** This is the set of views that, in one way or another, the real difference between art and bunk lies not so much in the work created but rather in the creator. It is how the object was meant or intended that settles the matter. Consequently what a work of art is, is secondary to the more important question of what an artist intends.

B. **Art and the audience.** This is the set of views that the difference between art and bunk lies in the nature of the audience that sees, hears or reads it. That either as individuals or collectively, consciously or unconsciously, it is the audience that decides what will count as the difference between art and bunk. And so there is no general or necessary distinction to be drawn. We all draw our own. In short, to paraphrase the popular dictum – art is in the eye of the beholder.

C. **Art and tradition.** Finally there is the set of views that the difference between art and bunk is to be found neither in the intentions of the artist nor in the responses of an audience but in something which determines the nature of both artist and audience. On this view, what, at any moment, counts as the difference between art and bunk is something determined by an historical process. In all its social, economic and cultural complexity, a work of art is an essentially historically conditioned object.

It is in terms of these three sorts of answer that we shall examine our question. Each chapter will explore one kind of answer, working through it to try to discern what there is of value in its approach.

To anticipate, our response to this question will locate the notion of a work of art at the intersection of two ideas, expressed in the following passages.

The philosopher Richard Wollheim writes:

> ...for the better understanding of this concept (of art) I shall leave you with an image. We may think of the concept of art as a protective parent. It is in its shadow that the vast oedipal conflict that is known as the history of art is fought out – a conflict in which the sons win, if they do, by becoming parents. Then they bear the concept that has borne them.

Minus the Freudian imagery, this is what we shall understand as the idea of a regulative concept of art. The contrast, as we shall see, is with accounts of the concept of art which regard it as essentially a static, ahistorical, descriptive, concept.

The second passage is from the work of the philosopher Stanley Cavell. He writes:

> In emphasizing the experiences of fraudulence and trust as essential to the experience of art, I am in effect claiming that the answer to the question 'What is art?' will in part be an answer which explains why it is we treat certain objects, or how we *can* treat certain objects, in ways normally reserved for treating persons.

The argument of this book will be that to understand how both these passages are true is at least to begin to understand the sort of differences there are between art and bunk.

where the questions bite

It is important to stress at the outset that the term 'work of art' as it is used in this book is not to be thought to be confined solely to the visual arts. Indeed, it will often be useful in the argument to show that we can avoid confusion concerning the works in a particular medium, – literature, drama (whether theatre, film or television), dance, and so on – by reflecting on the sort of thing we say about the works of other media. To this extent, then, the argument of this book attempts to resist the continuing and highly successful efforts of artists and critics in the visual arts to reserve the terms 'art' and 'work of art' entirely for their own use. Indeed, it is perhaps possible to trace many of the stranger philosophical fantasies that have haunted the visual arts in this century to the mistaken idea that artists in these media have sole responsibility for this vocabulary.

On the other hand, we shall take the visual arts as our primary area of concern. There are two reasons for doing this. First of all, as regards our enjoyment and appreciation of nature, most people feel most familiar with the idea of enjoying the visual appearance of natural objects or ensembles of such objects. Only in the visual arts do we find what seems to be a parallel insistence on the centrality of the appearance of physical objects, on how things look. Taking works in the visual arts as central examples, therefore, is a useful way of dram-atising one of the central ideas of the argument: the contrast between the appearance of one sort of object of aesthetic interest, including both natural and created objects, and the appearance of works of art. This distinction, and what it involves, will, it is hoped, be sharper against the background of superficial similarity.

The second reason for taking the visual arts as primary is this. With the possible exception of music, it is, in this century, artists in the visual arts who have set the highest stakes for the success or failure of their art. In the visual arts, perhaps as nowhere else, the criteria for what is to count as success or failure are most often themselves the explicit product of an individual artist's endeavours. It is here that we feel most keenly that either we are justified in refusing to accept the objects proffered as works of art, or that if we come to see the art in such objects we will no longer be certain about where we located the art in previous works. This is just what we feel about *Equivalent VIII*. In short, this is where the questions bite.

As the first step on our survey of these different views, we should introduce ourselves to the head of that family of concepts to which the notion of a 'work of art' belongs; the concept of the aesthetic. In particular, we must see just what the relation is between this concept and that of a work of art.

why should it matter?

To introduce ourselves to the concept of the aesthetic, let us ask this question. Why should anyone pay any attention to this matter of Andre and his bricks? Why on earth should it matter that we answer this question about the sort of difference there is between art and bunk?

The first reason is this. We are often told that what particular works of art mean is, or ought to be, of immense relevance to our lives. Nevertheless, artists, critics and philosophers often give the impression that understanding and enjoying the significance of such works involves the use of special skills, taking up special sorts of attitude, and having special sorts of experience, all of which are supposed to be largely unrelated to anything else we ordinarily do in life. Even when we are invited to think that there may be something important in common between, say, looking at an enthralling landscape painting and looking at an enthralling landscape, both are still thought of as relatively rare experiences isolated from everyday life.

But this is not right. Our enjoyment and appreciation of works of art in whatever medium is not something completely isolated from everyday aspects of human life. All of us, most of the time, make decisions, come to conclusions, and above all appreciate and enjoy things in ways which are the same sorts of ways in which we enjoy and understand works of art. What things? Almost anything. Consider some examples and reflect on the questions asked about them.

1. You have finally got round to redecorating the living room. But you cannot afford a new carpet. How can you

best create that fresh, airy atmosphere you would like when the carpet is so dark and dour?

2.   You have an important interview and you want to make the right impression. Which shoes do you wear with your suit?

3.   You are chatting with a friend. He tells a long anecdote about his last holiday. Your friend makes such a mess of telling it, jumping backwards and forwards, forgetting important bits and so on, that the 'punchline' is lost on you. In a way the story is quite funny but you don't laugh. Why?

4.   You decide to eat your lunch in the park today. Whereabouts do you sit?

5.   You are trying to get your children to keep their room tidy. But they say they like it as it is. What do you disagree about?

6.   You meet someone new. What do you think of them?

7.   You are walking on the beach. Suddenly you come across a plastic bag full of rotting refuse. What is your reaction? Why?

Such examples could be multiplied endlessly. This is just because they are drawn from the ordinary trivia of life. So too, the sort of answers that can be given to the questions asked above are endlessly various. They may involve very different factors like our image of ourselves, power, sexual attraction, our desire to impress and influence others, moral factors, economic factors and so on. But while all these sorts of considerations can enter into the response to such questions so too can another very different sort of consideration.

Consider the example of deciding where to sit in the park. It may be that you would like to sit under the trees because there is a chance of rain and the trees would afford some shelter. Or perhaps because you feel like remaining alone and undisturbed. Or even because from there you could see which of your colleagues has also come to the park – perhaps you would like to see how long they take for lunch. Note that in each of these cases you have something to gain – rest, shelter, a longer lunch break. However, it might also be that the reason that you would like to sit under the trees is because the park looks at its finest from that particular perspective.

Again, consider finding the pile of refuse on the beach. It may be that you object to this because you consider it a health hazard. Or because it makes you feel nauseous. Thus you might wish the refuse were not there in order not to be disadvantaged – by being made ill or by being injured. But it might also be because you think it spoils the appearance of the beach. In short, you object because it is ugly.

It is far from clear that there is any material advantage conferred simply by attending to such things as fine perspectives and by avoiding such things as ugly views. Yet clearly we do think that we have reasons for doing such things. This is shown by the fact that to the question, 'Why are you sitting there?' the answer, 'Because of the view' makes perfect sense.

aesthetic interests

Because of their difference from other sorts of reason, and from other sorts of interest in the world, it makes sense to group these sorts of reasons and these sorts of interests together. The term 'aesthetic' is simply a way of doing this. So insofar as your reason for sitting in a particular place in the park is because of the fine view this affords and insofar as you wish the rubbish were not on the beach because it spoils the appearance of the shoreline, your reasons are properly described as 'aesthetic'. Your interest in such things is also properly called an 'aesthetic' interest.

There are many other features of 'aesthetic' reasons and interests, other reasons why it makes sense to group certain activities and experiences together in this way. For example, it will perhaps be obvious already that in each of these examples the notion of how something *appears* or *seems* plays a central role. As we shall see, because of its important role, the notion of appearance is a most fertile source of confusion.

A feature of this idea of the aesthetic which is more relevant at the moment emerges directly from what has been said so far. As reflection on some of the examples above will testify, aesthetic concerns are not confined to the pleasing, the beautiful, or the interesting. We express our aesthetic preferences just as much in finding things unpleasant, ugly or boring. Dissatisfaction with the poorly-recounted anecdote, for example, is very often aesthetic dissatisfaction. This is because someone unable to tell a 'good story' does not lack the sort of skill that someone unable to speak French lacks. She lacks the sort of skill that someone unable to draw lacks.

The fact that our aesthetic preferences and concerns are also expressed in negative ways is very important. It is important because neglecting the fact that, for example, the distasteful, the banal and the tedious belong alongside the tasteful, the beautiful and the touching is one reason why we are sometimes prone to forget just how pervasive aesthetic interest is. And forgetting this is indeed one of the principal sources of misunderstanding about the notion of a work of art. In particular, it leads to the idea that questions about works of art are not important because they have nothing to do with ordinary life.

The problem is that we make the mistake of thinking that we are only engaged aesthetically with the world around us when we are deliberately attending to the Very Beautiful View or the Very Beautiful Object. We think of the aesthetic as the unique, as the special. And this means that we then forget just how much of the ordinary details of life are involved in making aesthetic decisions. Just how much, for example, the environment in which most of us live has been determined by the aesthetic decisions of ourselves and others. Further, we forget how much of our lives that has nothing to do with *looking at things* involves aesthetic concerns and preferences: the way we speak, being bored, enjoying sport, selling services of all kinds, how we get on or don't get on with our fellows. Very important to the way in which aesthetic interests are involved in social life is the idea of 'fit', of what we think of as appropriate or inappropriate congruence, between, for example, a person's character and the sort of thing that happens to him in his life. The sort of 'fit' which we may crudely describe as 'ironic' or 'tragic'. Or the sort of fit between different aspects of someone's life so that we describe it as being all of a piece. Or the relationships between facets of different people's characters. And so on.

All these activities and attitudes need not involve being aesthetically interested in objects but nevertheless they may be, and usually are, controlled and determined by aesthetic factors. All these everyday phenomena and more are what we should recall when we think of the role of the aesthetic in our lives.

It is important to understand this correctly. The point is not that the ordinary details of life are special, if only we see them correctly. This too may be an important idea but it is different from the one that now concerns us. The present point is that the ordinary trivia of life, whilst we still think of it as ordinary, is in large part ordinary *aesthetic* trivia.

While aesthetic responses in ordinary life may vary from culture to culture, we should be very surprised indeed to come across someone who, though he has occasion, takes no aesthetic interest at all in his environment. That someone might find the entire world aesthetically distasteful or boring is perhaps intelligible. But that someone with otherwise normal abilities, ample opportunity, freedom from distraction and so on should simply never understand the point of his fellow's aesthetic interest in *anything* borders on the unintelligible. Trying to make sense of such a case can show us just how deeply aesthetic interests are embedded in the sort of creature we are. Because of this, we are the sort of creature for whom the creation of artefacts, including works of art, that answer to such interests is a natural activity. In the end it is because of a fact of this sort that questions about works of art ought to matter to us.

arty facts
We now need to be more precise. Just what is the relation

between this notion of the aesthetic and that of a work of art? We shall now look at one popular conception of this relation and go on to argue that it cannot be right.

The popular conception runs something like this. There are fundamentally two sorts of objects which are aesthetically interesting. There are natural objects and there are artefacts. Works of art are a special class of artefact. They are special in that unlike many other artefacts which have been made to be useful or fulfil some function, works of art have been made especially to provoke and engage our aesthetic interest. Works of art are therefore definable as artefacts which have been deliberately made by people to provoke and engage the aesthetic interests of their fellows.

There are many theories of art which share the thought that this is the true definition of works of art. Some accounts – called 'Formalist' accounts – stress that nothing more is needed: that the point of producing such objects is exclusively to provoke such an interest. To others it has seemed that while works of art also have other functions, these vary over different times and cultures. For example, sometimes works of art have had a religious function; sometimes not. So works of art must be defined as objects created to provoke our aesthetic interest, not because this is all they ever do, but because this is the only thing we can say about works of art that is always and everywhere true.

But in many other theories of art the fundamental idea is supplemented with ideas about what this provocation and engagement of aesthetic interest must be made to do, what function or value it must have. The range of these supplementary ideas is extremely varied. The very general ideas that works of art exist must in some way 'enrich human experience' or 'express the artist's emotions', or even in some way 'liberate the human spirit' are claims familiar to most of us.

Naturally, there is a great deal of disagreement about these supplementary ideas. Such disputes are often taken to support the idea that what counts as a work of art is relative to particular historical or cultural conditions. We will look at this view in Chapter 4 and as we proceed will refer again to the particular additional claims made by different theories. The point for now is that, by and large, most traditional accounts of the notion of a work of art have the same sort of shape.

What these theories of art have in common is that they all agree that this description is correct; that works of art are simply artefacts deliberately made to provoke and engage aesthetic interest. They disagree about whether and how this description needs to be filled out to include the function or value of this provocation and engagement. If only this could be agreed, then they will have described the concept of a work of art. These theories, then, claim that the notion of art we use is simply one which describes a certain sort of object.

Many critics, artists and philosophers think this way. But there are good reasons for believing that they ought not to do so. Indeed, it is the central claim of this book that it is thinking in just this sort of way about the notion of a work of art that leads us into such confusion when we consider Andre's bricks; that makes us unable to answer the question about the sort of difference there is between art and bunk.

The reason why it is a mistake to think of works of art in this way, is that this fails to take account of a crucial difference. This difference concerns not the fact of whether or not the object was made by someone but the role that knowing this fact plays in how we understand the object. The difference is between objects which have been made to provoke aesthetic interest and about which it is important to know that they were made for this reason and objects which have been made to provoke aesthetic interest and about which we do not need to know that they were made at all. Once we appreciate this distinction, we see the need for a very different approach to the concept of a work of art. We will have to stop thinking of the notion of a work of art that we use as one which is solely descriptive. Since this distinction is so important in this inquiry, we will take this first justification of the contrast stage by stage.

The opening stage is to remind ourselves that we do not, as is so often thought, simply distinguish between aesthetically interesting natural objects and aesthetically interesting artefacts.

nature isn't art...

First of all it is important to note that we do distinguish between natural objects of aesthetic interest and works of art. As some of the earlier examples remind us, many aspects and features of the natural world are of immense aesthetic interest. Typically, it is the dramatic or the exotic in nature which springs most readily to mind – Ayers Rock, the Grand Canyon, a spectacular sunset and so on. But we also find great pleasure on a smaller and more transitory scale. The striking appearance of a pebble found on a stroll, the light catching a sparrow's eye, the cloud formation that, just for a moment, seems like someone one knows. Perhaps less frequent is the sort of interest we can take in the otherwise indifferent and mundane, even in what is conventionally thought of as ugly, tedious or distasteful. This is perhaps more familiar to us in terms of the human environment. How many of us have not been struck on some occasion by, say, the particular look of a torn wrapper in the street? Or by the sound of rain on that old sheet of corrugated iron, or even by the drama of a semi-ritualised drunken row outside the railway station, late at night? Our attitude at such moments may lend support to the view mentioned earlier that it is important to enliven our sense of the specialness, the sacredness even, of the familiar and of the ordinary.

However, despite the enormous, necessary, aesthetic interest we take in different features of the natural world, no one would seriously hold that we regard such features as works of art. So, of course, we distinguish between natural objects of aesthetic interest and works of art. But if so, we must believe that if we respond to something aesthetically, it does not follow that what we are responding to must be a work of art.

...nor is your bedroom

We must now note that this is true even when we are concerned not with natural objects but with aesthetically interesting artefacts. Moreover, and this is the important claim, it does not follow that something is a work of art even if it is an artefact that we have made in order to provoke or satisfy aesthetic interests and preferences.

Take, for example, decorating one's bedroom. Clearly, just because it turns out to be of some aesthetic interest – it ends up with a certain sort of charm – it does not follow that the room is a work of art. Aesthetic concerns may have played no part in the decoration at all.

Certainly, it is true that aesthetic preferences usually do enter into the decoration of rooms. We may have arrived at the final result through making a wide range of aesthetic comparisons, the overall effect being judged by how successfully the room meets the aesthetic ends we had in mind. But, again, it does not follow from this that the newly decorated room is a work of art. We do not generally regard even finely decorated rooms in this way. This does not mean that there can't be rooms which can be appropriately regarded as works of art. It means that just because something is produced with

It does not follow that the room is a work of art.

some aesthetic end in mind and is of aesthetic interest, perhaps of immense interest, it does not follow that it must be a work of art.

What follows from this is that, even after we have put talk of the function of art to one side, there must be more to being a work of art than simply being an artefact produced with aesthetic ends in mind. Identifying this difference is the job of the next stage of the argument.

light in the forest

Imagine that somewhere in a forest, in a sunlit clearing, there stands a magnificent tree. It is truly a beautiful sight. Imagine that the clearing has a series of somewhat prolix visitors. If, for example, a forester discovers the clearing then she might say something like this:

> What a beautiful example of *Quercus Marilandica*! The Black-jack Oak. Notice how the branch structure allows the maximum spread with the minimum risk of wind damage. And this structure is of course echoed in the roots below. Yes, this particular tree exemplifies the biological principles perfectly. A really fine *Quercus Marilandica*!

For the forester, then, the tree in the clearing is a fine example of a particular type. For her it is a beautiful thing when considered as an example of the Blackjack Oak.

Now imagine that a wildlife enthusiast enters the clearing. He might say:

> What a beautiful oak! Just think of how long it has stood here – centuries! Think of the life that it has contained and supported. The generations of squirrels that have lived within it. The birds that have nested in its branches. The creatures that feed on its seed. And how all of this fits together in harmonious order. It is not just a tree – it's a world!

For the wildlife enthusiast, then, the tree in the clearing is beautiful because of what it does and for the life it supports. For him it is a beautiful thing when considered as a ecosystem.

If we go on to imagine now that there comes to the clearing a child who loves climbing, or some lovers on a stroll or an elderly carpenter, we can see that all of them might agree that the tree in the clearing was beautiful, but considered as something quite different in each case.

Imagine next that you yourself come to the clearing. You say:

> What a beautiful sight! The greens! The light! The grace of that branch that almost meets the ground. The English Oak – a really beautiful thing.

For you, the tree in the clearing is beautiful considered as – what? Well considered as nothing in particular. Just as a thing, as a sight, considered as something to see. You don't even know what sort of tree it is. ('A Blackjack by any other name...'). What engages your interest is how the thing, whatever it is, looks to you at that moment. Unlike the others, you might have a completely different reaction if, say, it began to rain or the light changed.

Imagine further, that we were now to tell all the visitors to the clearing that though the tree looks very like a Blackjack Oak, it is in fact a rather inferior example of a Chinese Pi Tree. And, as everyone knows, the Chinese Pi, though it can in the right conditions grow to look uncannily like an Blackjack Oak, even fooling experienced foresters, has stinging leaves which are poisonous to all life and its wood is impossible to work.

It should be clear that you will be the only person who will still judge that the thing in the clearing is beautiful for the same reason. Of course, it may be that knowing it is a dangerous Chinese Pi so disturbs you that you are unable to see it in quite the same way. But it is still the case that what you found attractive about the tree in the clearing did not depend upon it being anything in particular: whether it was an English Oak tree or not, it was still a beautiful sight. This would be so even if there were in fact no real tree at all in the clearing, if it were just an extremely curious illusion, a hologram perhaps. You would have every right to be thoroughly perplexed but you would still have no reason to retract your judgement. Illusions can be very beautiful!

Your interest in the tree, then, is the case of an aesthetic interest in an object which does not depend upon thinking of the object as of a particular kind, or as having some function. Your interest in it is completely independent of any thought of its origins or its true nature. There is a widely held view that only this sort of interest is genuine aesthetic interest; that there is genuine aesthetic interest only if we are interested solely in the appearance of an object, how the object is experienced by the observer; that therefore interest in anything other than this is not aesthetic interest at all. We will need to keep returning to this view as we proceed. For when applied to works of art, it is the mirror image of the approach we really need.

Tadzio and tigers

But for the moment, we should turn to examine those occasions where it is essential that the object of our aesthetic interest is being considered as something of a particular kind.

For example, imagine walking along the street and being suddenly stopped in your tracks by the sight of a really wonderful face. Perhaps the face of a man or woman with the conventionalized beauty of the late 80s' fashion model, or the unique perfection of the boy Tadzio from *Death In Venice.*

Now to find a particular man, woman or child beautiful or striking in this way is to find him or her beautiful as a man, woman or child. If it were possible to regard a child's face simply as a visual appearance, as a set of loosely related patches of colour and texture, then Tadzio might well have been more aesthetically pleasing if only his features had not been quite so fine but were, say, a little weathered. The 'ivory-white' of his face might be less attractive than a browner hue. But of course, at this, an Aschenbach will simply smile and walk away. To see the boy's face in this abstract way is to miss everything. What is unique about Tadzio just is his appearance as a beautiful child. More rugged features would simply ruin this. Similar considerations apply in the case of fashion models. In these cases, seeing the wonder of the face necessarily means considering it as a wonderful face. If it turns out to be not the face of a person but just a clever dummy or automaton then it may not be wonderful in any way at all.

Conversely, I may properly find something ugly or

unattractive which might, if it were not necessary to think of it *as* something, have been beautiful. Thus, lines and patterns which might have been quite charming on their own, would probably appear quite loathsome if branded onto someone's body. And as some modern architects are at last being informed, buildings which might be very fine considered as exemplifications of solutions to mathematical, political or financial problems may appear quite different when we reflect that we have to think of them as places in which people must live or work.

Again, considered in themselves, many horses might appear attractive were it not the case that we must think of them as racehorses or workhorses or pets. In all these cases, our interest depends upon considering the things as something of a particular kind.

Comparing this last example with the way in which we find, say, tigers aesthetically attractive should give a good grasp of the distinction we need to make. Unlike tigers, horses have been invested by us with all manner of tasks and functions which, to some degree, differ from culture to culture. This means that when we consider how attractive a particular horse is, we consider it in some particular respect. Thus, while we might well hold that all horses are beautiful, judgements of the beauty of a particular horse are usually expressed in the form 'What a beautiful horse!' Whereas, when we say 'Gosh! What a beautiful tiger!' we usually mean 'The tiger; what a beautiful thing!' Otherwise we should have to say something like 'I've seen a great many of them you know and I can tell you that this tiger really is something special!'

what makes a work of art different
We have seen that we do not simply distinguish between natural objects of aesthetic interest and created objects of aesthetic interest. For we also distinguish between artefacts made to provoke aesthetic interest and works of art. There must be a further difference.

We have now developed a way of identifying this further difference. It is between finding something aesthetically attractive (or not), period, and finding something aesthetically attractive (or not) as something. The really important point to note about this distinction is that, as the examples given suggest, it cuts across that between natural objects and artefacts. Both natural objects and artefacts may be considered aesthetically interesting as things of a particular kind, in the light of their origins or function. And both natural objects and artefacts may be thought aesthetically interesting apart from any thought of their origins or function.

This means that if, for example, we happen to find the curve of the handle of a favourite old knife, caught in a shaft of light, suddenly captivating, it does not matter to us at that moment that the curve is deliberately designed to enable the knife to be comfortable to use. Insofar as we are interested in the handle of the knife simply for how it appears to us, the knife may as well be a natural object. What it does, or how it came to be, is simply not relevant to this sort of interest in it.

On the other hand, if what we find aesthetically interesting is the design of the knife, how gracefully it handles and cuts, then we must be attending to what the object is and what it is supposed to do.

What about works of art? Is our interest in works of art of the kind where we need to ignore origins and functions or of the kind where we must take them into account? Or can it, as in the cases of our interest in some natural objects and some artefacts other than works of art, be of either kind depending upon the circumstances? Here is the essential difference between, on the one hand, natural and man-made objects of aesthetic appreciation and on the other, works of art.

Unlike natural and some man-made objects of aesthetic appreciation, in the case of works of art, it always matters, aesthetically, that we know what kind of thing the object is. In particular, it matters, aesthetically, that we know that it was made. It is never the case that we can properly be indifferent to the origins of a work of art, to the fact that it was made, and yet be aesthetically interested in it. If we were indifferent to this, we would be attending to the wrong thing – we would not be attending aesthetically to the work.

moore than a meteorite

To see this, consider the case of a Moore and a meteorite. Imagine that into an outdoor exhibition of Henry Moore pieces there falls a meteorite. A meteorite that happens exactly to resemble one of the pieces on display. This is perhaps not so fantastic. After all, Moore always claimed how central to his work was the need to echo and embrace naturally occurring forms of figure and landscape. Imagine that the two objects are placed side by side. What does it make sense to say of each of them? Try the exercise on the next page.

There are, of course, many concepts that are applicable to both objects. But most of these terms are not amongst them: there aren't many terms in this list that we can cross through. Unless you are thinking about one of the objects as something that was made, it does not make sense to ask, for example, whether or not that object is witty, or simplistic, or crass, or vulgar. And so on. The fact that some of these terms are clearly inappropriate to describe the meteorite shows that to think of an object as a work of art is to attend to an object in a quite different way from the way we attend to natural objects.

To be prepared to see something as a work of art, then, is to be prepared to see entirely different *sorts* of things in the object from what we are prepared to see if it is, or may as well be, a natural object. We are interested in its intelligence, humour, insight and so on. Once we see, say, the wit in a piece of a sculpture, it is incomprehensible to us that this sort of quality should be thought irrelevant to someone's interest in it. We have only to think of works in other media, of poems, dances and pieces of music, to realise how much we would have to ignore if we treated them as if they were only incidentally made by someone.

So what we are responding to when we consider an object as a work of art is the appearance of the object as meant by someone. We are interested in its appearance as a work. We are not interested in it as an object, which, just as a matter of fact, happens to have been made by someone but which might as well have been a natural object.

A. Recumbent Figure (1938). Henry Moore.

B. Meteorite. Fell from sky.

Assume that (a) A and B are physically identical; (b) you know which is which.

Try crossing through those terms which *could* be true of both A and B. For example, if you think that both Henry Moore's sculpture and the meteorite *could* be graceful (even if you don't think either actually is) then cross through 'graceful'.

Elegant	Balanced	Controlled	Vulgar	Lifelike
Dainty	Heavy	Courageous	Crass	Charged
Graceful	Smooth	Responsible	Glib	Romantic
Poised	Bland	Insightful	Absurd	Overnice
Clumsy	Interesting	Intelligent	Heavy handed	Dramatic
Dumpy	Boring	Wise	Witty	Classical
Natural	Fine featured	Childish	Simplistic	Moving

Moore and the meteorite.

a rule, not a label

This conclusion has important implications for our whole inquiry. One thing it shows is this. We do not – cannot – simply stumble across objects, inspect them and then conclude that they are or are not works of art. Rather, in order to be able to see something as a work of art, as something whose appearance was intended for an aesthetic end, I must bring the notion of a work of art along with me and use it to guide what I see in the object. In short, to be able to see the intended appearance of the object, I must already be prepared to see it as a work of art. This means that to call something a work of art is not to express a conclusion about the object. It is to announce that, insofar as we are aesthetically interested in this object, it is not simply its physical appearance to which we must attend. The notion of a work of art is not a tag we place on the object after the main event. It is the programme for the main event. It is not merely a label. It is much more like a rule. The concept of a work of art does not describe: it regulates.

Examples from other media, other sorts of works of art, may make this clearer. Nobody who sees *The Merchant of Venice* ought to think that Shylock is Jewish merely by chance. And that now they will just watch what happens to him. As I will now watch what happens to the man who crosses the street outside my window who may also happen to be Jewish. In the case of Shylock, it is in part to his being Jewish, but also to everything else about him, that it is intended that I should pay attention. Again, one does not listen to music in the same way that one listens to the sound of the waves. For even when music imitates natural sounds it is intended to do so, and so what we listen to is the intended-to-be-natural sound. This affects how we listen to it.

In this respect the visual arts are no different. What we attend to is not just the physical appearance of the stone or the visual appearance of the paint on the canvas, though of course we must attend to such things. But, if we must do so, we must do so in order to attend to the intended appearance. It is the intended appearance which is the relevant object of aesthetic interest.

So, unlike other artefacts which may be deliberately produced to provoke aesthetic interest, works of art are capable of rewarding aesthetic interest in *why* they appear as they do. They are therefore capable not only of being aesthetically interesting, but also of being aesthetically *intelligible*.

And this is why a set of fire-bricks in a builders' yard may be striking or bland. But the same set of bricks in a gallery may be revolutionary or banal.

As this suggests, we will find in what follows that thinking of the concept of a work of art as a regulative, rather than a descriptive, term is the key to unlocking the sort of difference there is between art and bunk. For now we should note one minor, but very helpful, consequence of what has been said.

On the argument so far, to say that an artefact made with aesthetic ends in mind is not a work of art is not to judge it aesthetically worthless. For as we have seen, a work of art is not simply an artefact designed with aesthetic ends in mind. It therefore does not matter that such artefacts are not works of art. Indeed, it is possible that there are very many artefacts which are more valuable in respect of important sorts of aesthetic interest than very many works of art. Recalling this more often might help to produce both more interesting artefacts and more intelligible works of art.

summary

We have seen that artists can present us with objects which force us to ask if we still know what we mean when we think and talk about works of art. In order to be able to determine what sort of a difference there is between a work of art and anything else, between art and bunk, it was said to be necessary to familiarise ourselves with a family of concepts, chief of which is that of the aesthetic. We saw how pervasive is the need for this concept.

However, the relationship between this idea of the aesthetic and that of a work of art is not so straightforward as it might first appear. It might seem that a work of art is simply an object that has been deliberately made so that its appearance may provoke aesthetic interest. Some theories of art add elements to this definition. But it still remains the case on these theories that the only difference between natural objects and works of art is that the appearance of the latter has been deliberately created.

However, when we came to look more closely at our enjoyment and appreciation of natural objects we come across a crucial distinction. This is between finding something aesthetically interesting (or not) for how it appears to us and finding something aesthetically interesting (or not) when it is considered as something in particular.

We then saw that this suggests that a work of art is not merely an object that provokes aesthetic interest and happens to have been deliberately made by somebody to do just that. Rather, the knowledge that a work of art was made by somebody is essential to its being properly understood and enjoyed. This means that its having been made by someone is an essential ingredient in the way it appears to us. When we talk about the appearance of a work of art we do not mean just how that particular physical object appears to us at some particular moment. If we did, the work might as well be a natural object. Rather it is the intended appearance which is the object of aesthetic interest. The work is the object as meant.

This makes possible questions about why it was so intended. It is this insight, about the connection between artistic intention and aesthetic intelligibility, that we carry with us into the next chapter.

notes

p.1. *Equivalent VIII* is fully catalogued in the *Biennial Report, The Tate Gallery 1972-4*. Critical acclaim for Andre's work is widespread but see especially 'The Razed Sites of Carl Andre', David Bourdon, *Artforum* (October, 1966) and Richard Morphet's 'Carl Andre's Bricks', *The Burlington Magazine*, no. 884 (November, 1976) pp. 762-7. This latter was a reply to the sharply critical editorial in the same magazine in April, 1976. Other notable attacks of the time include Bernard Levin's column in *The Times* 18th February, 1976. See also 'An Interview with Carl Andre' in *Beyond the Crisis in Art*, Peter Fuller (London, Writers and Readers Publishing Co-operative Society Ltd, 1980) pp. 110-34. The definitive catalogue of Andre's work to date is *Carl Andre – Stedelijk Van Abbemuseum Eindhoven & Gemeentemuseum Den Hagg*, (Eindhoven, 1987).

p.8. The passage by Richard Wollheim is from 'The Art Lesson' and can be found in *On Art and the Mind - Essays and Lectures*, Richard Wollheim (London, Allen Lane, 1973) p. 151. The idea of a regulative use for a concept of art is drawn from 'A Conversation with Richard Wollheim' in *Modern British Philosophy*, Bryan Magee (Herts., Paladin, 1973) pp. 220-35, especially p. 224. This piece and Wollheim's work in general has been influential throughout the book.

p.9. The passage by Stanley Cavell is from his essay 'Music Dis-composed' in *Must We Mean What We Say?*, Stanley Cavell (Cambridge, Cambridge University Press, 1976) p. 189. Again the influence of this piece and Cavell's work in general runs right through the book. Also helpful in this context is 'Understanding People and Understanding Art', B.R. Tilghman, *Proceedings of the 8th International Wittgenstein Symposium, 1983* (Vienna, Holder Pichler Temsky, 1984) pp. 153-59.

p.15. The best known formalist theory of art is the doctrine of 'significant form' found in *Art*, Clive Bell (London, Chatto and Windus, 1914).

p.16. A useful anthology of classic theories of art is *Philosophy of Art and Aesthetics – From Plato to Wittgenstein*, ed. Frank A. Tillman and Steven M. Cahn (London, Harper and Row, 1969).

p.19. The following discussion is a rough paraphrase of Kant's 1790 distinction between free and dependent beauty in the great classic of aesthetics *The Critique of Aesthetic Judgement* (Oxford, Oxford University Press, 1980) especially Section 16. Also influential through-out the book is Section 45.

2: art and the artist

Is the difference between art and bunk there to be seen (or for that matter, heard, or read or touched), if we are only alive to it? Or does this difference consist in something that, as it were, lies. behind the object: its origins, its context of production, the reasons for which it was made? In particular, is it what the artist intended to do which makes the real difference?

It first needs to be said that, of course, we may well be interested in the thoughts, feelings and intentions of particular artists in the way we are interested in those of Napoleon, Mother Teresa or Mikhail Gorbachev. We may be, and often are, interested in the artist as a striking and unusual sort of person. This is simply because, over and above the fact that they spend a great deal of time and energy making and thinking about making works of art, artists very often are striking people leading unorthodox, intense or otherwise out of the ordinary lives. So we may be interested in an artist for these perfectly legitimate sorts of reasons. But this cannot be the sort of interest with which we are concerned here. We are concerned with the different question of what role the artist's intentions makes to our evaluation of the works of art that he makes. So the question we need to look at is not whether it matters, in any way at all, what the artist intended to do when he made this work of art. For it might matter in all sorts of ways. But does it matter *aesthetically* what the artist intended to do?

That this is crucial to how we should understand works of art is in accord with many of our intuitions about our experience of them. We often feel, for example, that in coming to be familiar with a great canon of work, with a set of symphonies, or a series of plays or poems, or a collection of paintings ranging over different times and themes, we are through them coming to be familiar with something which lies behind them, because of which they are what they are. This is the spirit or mind of the artist. And it is characteristic of this experience that we come to think that the works have the value they do because of this relation to the life of their creator. A peculiarly intimate relation which we have only to our voices or to our bodies.

When we reflect on this, we are encouraged to think that the notion of a work of art is parasitic upon that of an artist; that works of art are artefacts produced by a special sort of person and that thereby they acquire a special sort of character. And it is because of this, we may think, that it is possible to make sense of the idea of the life of a work of art and to think of this life as one of thought and feeling.

In the preceding chapter we saw that the boring and the banal are also expressions of aesthetic interest. So, here too, where we find a body of work that strikes us as dull, or crass,

Coming to be familiar with the spirit of the artist.

or derivative, we are prone to describe this in terms of the artist's narrowness of vision, or lack of originality, or intellectual or spiritual torpidity. And we may say that what is missing is the right sort of relation between the look of the objects produced and the aims of the artist who made them; that the intention was not to express but only to impress; to play a puerile game with the current fashions of the day. Or perhaps to demonstrate a purely technical expertise. And we may be inclined to say that individuals who are prone to such temptations will never have what is needed to produce works of art. In short, we may think, bunk is as the member for Buncombe does.

trick or treat?
We often appeal to just such views about the character of works of art when we disagree about whether something is art or bunk in a particular case. Those convinced that *Equivalent VIII* is at best a joke and at worst a fraud will claim that the proponents of the opposing view recklessly ascribe serious artistic motives, intellectual rigour, or a profound grasp of form and feeling where none of these things are to be found. For them Andre is a joker or a fraudster. On the other hand, Andre's supporters will regard his detractors as carelessly ignorant of the relevant background of thought and motive. Andre is serious, innovative, classical even, steeped in the traditions of his chosen medium. Note that both hold that the facts of what Andre intended to do are crucial. For it is the nature of these intentions that determines what it will be true to say of the object.

But if these facts about the artist really do constitute the difference which concerns us, then this has some interesting implications for the audiences of art. For in the same way that deceitful behaviour may look like sincere behaviour, so it will be possible for objects which are not works of art to be treated as if they were indeed works of art. And just as it is possible to malign others by ascribing the wrong motives to their actions, so it will be possible to misjudge a work of art through ignorance of its origins. There is therefore never a guarantee that, by attending to the appearance of an object, an audience will be able to determine if the object truly belongs with works of art.

Take the forged banknote as an analogy. A forged note is not counterfeit because it does not look sufficiently like the genuine article, but because it was not made under the right authority. It is a note with the wrong history. But whether or not a note has the right or the wrong history is not something one can read on its face. However perfect his banknote, the forger relies on this fact. The difference between real and counterfeit notes is not a matter of how they look.

If what the artist intended is crucial, the same is true of works of art. The difference between art and bunk is external to appearance.

And this now reflects on the original positions of our critical protagonists. Those who are prone to regard *Equivalent VIII* as just a pile of bricks must admit that, if only the appropriate background of thought and feeling were supplied, if Andre were serious and correct in his grasp of a thriving medium, then it would be possible to treat it as a work of art. Conversely, those who are now prone to treat *Equivalent VIII* as a work of art, must admit that with different intentions implicated in its production, if Andre were fraudulent or ignorant or confused, it would indeed be just a pile of bricks. This is a consequence of making the concept of a work of art subservient to that of an artist, of holding that the origins of a object in the intentions of an artist are central to our conception of that object as a work of art.

Now we can come to understand both what is true and what is false in this view by seeing how well it withstands attack. We will do this by looking at two opposed views of the aesthetic importance of the artist's intentions. First, we shall examine the view that what the artist intended is irrelevant because while the intentions may be the cause of the work of art's appearance, they are not themselves part of that appearance. They are therefore not relevant objects of aesthetic attention.

Second, we shall discuss the view that if what the artist intended is relevant, this is so only because it is already the object of aesthetic attention. We cannot therefore seek to justify what we say about the work by appealing to what the artist intended.

Both views try to capture in different ways another set of intuitions about our experience of art: that there is a particular reason why we cannot make the worth of works of art a hostage to the circumstances of its production. The reason is that the worth of works of art is embedded in, and only in, how they appear to us.

two misconceptions

Before we examine these views, however, it is as well to get a couple of things clear about the nature of intention in this context.

First of all, to say of an artist that he intended to create this particular look to his work is not necessarily to say that before starting to paint, he engaged in an interior monologue with himself, formulating a description of the painting he wished to make which he then followed like a recipe, or imagining a picture in his head which he then copied. Nor, if we deny that this monologue occurred or that this mental picture existed, must we say that therefore the work was produced unconsciously or automatically.

Take, for example, the work of Jackson Pollock. It is not true, as was claimed by those who derided his paintings as the work of a 'Jack the Dripper', that because Pollock could not have envisaged just how they would turn out, these works were not produced deliberately or intentionally, but accidentally or casually. But nor is it the case, as some of those who admired Pollock's work claimed, that if he had no clear conception of the paintings before he began, and yet he produced them, the paintings must have been produced unconsciously or as the result of some mysterious, trance-like state of automatism, as if he were following a secret recipe or a hidden picture.

Pollock was neither a charlatan nor a shaman. As often occurs, people find something carried out or undergone by artists suspect and fraudulent, or else queer and mysterious, which in relevantly similar circumstances, outside the practice of art, is regarded as perfectly commonplace and straight-forward. At least, no trickery or mystery peculiar to art is involved.

I may go for a walk in town with no clear plan in mind, deciding only as I go along which direction to take next. It can yet happen that afterwards I can be seen to have to taken the most interesting way to walk around town, if I want to buy these things and avoid seeing those things. And I can be held to have intentionally taken that route around town. Which is to say that if you ask me why I took that route, I may be able to give you my reasons. Or I may not be able to give reasons but to the question 'How can someone who wanders around like that get all that he needs to buy this week?' I can answer, 'I've lived here a long time; I know this town.'

That the same is true in the case of artistic intention is evident as soon as we reflect that, certainly in the case of Jackson Pollock's paintings, making such works involved leaving marks, erasing marks and covering over marks just as much as simply making them. Such things cannot be planned in advance, either consciously or unconsciously. But they are done intentionally all the same. In the case of the painter's decisions, the thinking and the painting are at the end of the brush.

If we get confused about this, we become prey to a second misconception. This is the idea that a painting can come to mean something simply because it was intentionally made in a certain way. Simply because it was made with meaning in mind.

For example, people often think that *simply because of the way they were made*, Pollock's paintings are about action or the physicality of the act of painting or ritual or something similar. But this is false.

To see this, reflect that if we were to accept at face value the 'action-painting' interpretation, prevalent at one time, of Pollock's work, then it would be perverse to regard the paintings as works of art. For if what was really essential and significant was the existential or ritualistic character of the way Pollock worked, then it would have been the various acts of painting that constituted the Pollock canon and not the paintings them-selves. Or if permanence was still deemed to be important, then the films of Pollock painting would be his works. But whatever their documentary interest and, just considered as objects, their aesthetic interest, it is on this interpretation simply inconsistent to value paintings like *Lavender Mist* as works of art. The paintings themselves must be thought of as mere records or traces of the real works.

Compare footprints in the French chalk after the dance. We would think it odd to value such marks aesthetically because they were made as the result of the dance. This would be odd even though such footprints might make all sorts of interesting patterns and might allow us to make all sorts of inferences about the movements that must have been made to produce them.

A distinction often useful elsewhere in philosophy may be of some limited help here. As some philosophers have pointed out, there is an important set of differences between saying 'That sky *means* rain' and saying 'That flag *means* the race is off'. For our purposes the relevant difference is this. The first sense of 'meaning', called 'natural meaning', carries only a sense of causal association. That sky 'means' rain only in the sense that a cloudy sky like that is usually the cause of rain.

But the other sense of 'mean', called 'non-natural meaning', is quite different. Nobody thinks that waving the flag is the cause of the race having to be cancelled. The cause was an accident round the next bend. The waving of the flag carries the meaning that the race is now off. One explanation of how this is possible is that the flag waver intends that, in seeing him wave the flag, others will recognise that he intends them to believe that the race has been called off.

So the fact that the way a painting looks means (naturally) that it was made in a certain way, does not entail that what the painting means (non-naturally) is to do with how it was made. And this is true even if it was intentionally made in this way. The bare fact that Pollock's paintings were made in a ritualistic way does not even enable us, let alone constrain us, to see them as works of ritual.

Reflection on an analogy with our relations with each other may also prove helpful here. Imagine asking of someone how it was that he came to be sitting here. He might reply: 'Oh well, to cut a long story short, my cerebral cortex sent some signals to my motor function centres which in turn made my legs move which...' and so on. Certainly this, in one sense, captures how it was that he came to be sitting here. But it is very unlikely that it gives us what we wanted to know. What we usually want is an answer like 'Oh it's a long story but in brief, my Uncle lives in Antwerp. Now he thought that since I own a pet shop...' and so on. Or even something like 'Oh well – I just like sitting you know; I do a lot of it...'. These are answers that give not just causes and an account of how things were but reasons and an account of how things were for someone.

Similarly, someone may say that *Lavender Mist* looks as it does because Pollock put his canvas flat on the floor and then, paintpot in hand, walked around it and over it and so on. This may tell us how, causally, the painting came to look as it does. But just on its own, it tells us nothing about what we probably need help with. What, aesthetically, we need to understand is not that the work looks that way because of the way it was made. We need to understand how the work looks, by seeing why it was made that way.

So, in the sense in which his paintings have meaning, Pollock's paintings do not mean what they do *just* because they were intentionally made in a certain way, just because they were made with meaning in mind. Whatever his paintings are, they are because Jackson Pollock knew his craft.

In what follows, then, we should remember that artistic intention is not just a matter of meaning what one paints. It is a matter also of being able to paint what one means. And this is not to say that the sort of meaning that works of art have is like the meaning carried by a waving flag. Only that it isn't like the meaning of a thundery sky. With these thoughts in place, we can continue.

intentions are irrelevant
The first line of attack on the idea that the concept of artistic intention is central to that of a work of art is connected with that widespread conception of the character of works of art that we discussed and criticised earlier and that will have a part to play throughout our inquiry: the view that the essential truth

about works of art is that they are objects deliberately made for aesthetic ends. We can now examine this connection.

The two views are linked because they are both generated by the idea that to attend aesthetically to an object is to attend to the appearance of that object. More accurately, they are generated by having this thought, which in itself is correct, and then taking the notion of appearance, which is at its centre, as simple and straightforward. As we will now see, the argument then trades on the fact that, while what an artist intends can be the cause of an object's appearance, it can never be part of the content of that appearance.

The relevant line of thought might run something like this. We ask first: why should the fact that something was made by someone matter aesthetically?

To begin with it may be admitted that, certainly, this matters for some purposes. If we treated works of art as if they were just natural objects, then many things which surround the phenomenon of art would not exist. There would for example not be a history of art, which is to say, a kind of history which has at its centre the idea of how particular sorts of objects of aesthetic interest have changed over time. For though there is a history of how people have changed in their aesthetic responses to natural objects, there is no history of how natural objects have changed aesthetically. And so, if we treated works of art as if they were natural objects then there would be no discipline called the history of art.

But, the line of thought continues, it is far from obvious that there being a history of art is something essential to our experience of works of art. For, interesting though it may be, the history of art is not necessarily aesthetically interesting. It may be an important field of knowledge and inquiry without being aesthetically important.

Indeed, if the business of aesthetics is attention to the appearances of things, then the importance we give to the idea of the history of art, with its movements and fashions, its emphasis on originality and novelty, its concern with the actual conditions of production of those objects in the appearance of which we are interested, can only distract us from the real business of enjoying works of art for their own sake. If we consider originality in particular, it is clear that such a property concerns the relation of the object to other objects of the same type. Hence originality cannot be part of what we are interested in when we are interested in the appearance of the object alone. That Picasso's *Les Demoiselles d'Avignon* was highly original in form, no one ought to doubt. But equally no one ought to affirm that originality could be part of that form. Originality can never in itself be an aesthetic property.

The thought here is that since we have no need of a notion of the geological origins of the natural landscape before us, in order to find its appearance aesthetically enjoyable, we also have no need of the notion of the historical origins of the object when we look instead at a painting of that landscape, say one by Turner. We may of course know that a particular artist called Turner made this particular object. But it would not, aesthetically, matter in the least if we did not happen to know this fact. It would not matter if we did not know that the object had been made at all.

Surely, the line of thought might continue, a Turner painting would look the same if, however unlikely this was, it had been produced by the wind in an untidy corner of a paint factory. This would indeed be nothing short of a miraculous event and that it had occurred would make a difference to our interest in the object. But why should it make an aesthetic difference? If it is true, that to attend aesthetically to an object is to attend to the appearance of the object, then it is how the object now looks that is important; not how it came to look the way that it does. So it does not matter that the object looks the way it does because it was intended to look that way. And hence, the intentions of the artist, though of course causally efficacious in the production of the aesthetically interesting object, are not themselves part of its aesthetic interest. Aesthetically, they are irrelevant. What the artist intended is the object not of aesthetic interest but only of gratitude, surprise or, perhaps, regret.

the paste decorative diamond
The line of thought under examination, then, is one which seeks

to persuade us that we can safely eliminate the artist's intentions in producing a work of art from inclusion in what can count as an object of aesthetic interest. It seeks to do this by arguing that this is a direct consequence of the fact that only appearances are proper objects of aesthetic interest. The origins of the object, including its origins in the character, experience and intentions of the artist, are simply not to be found within such appearances.

It follows that, insofar as we seek to distinguish between art and bunk, that difference is to be described in terms of the physical appearance of the work and its aesthetic qualities. If Andre's *Equivalent VIII* is bunk, it is because of the aesthetic properties of that arrangement of bricks. In the visual arts, bunk is a matter of what things look like.

This conclusion is diametrically opposed to the one we encountered at the beginning of the chapter. On that view, those who are prone to regard *Equivalent VIII* as just a pile of bricks must admit that if its origins had been different, perhaps very different, it would be possible to treat it as a work of art. And vice-versa. The appropriate analogy for the difference between art and bunk was that between the genuine and the counterfeit banknote. Therefore the difference between art and bunk was not something that could be written on the face of the objects concerned.

Here the appropriate analogy is not the counterfeit note but the paste decorative diamond. If under examination in all conditions, paste and genuine gems really did appear the same, then at least for many people their difference in origin would count as nothing. If everyone acted (and, economics being what it is, could expect others to act) in the same way, the price of real diamond jewellery would fall. Apart from pure scarcity value, the important difference between real and imitation gems is how they look.

Similarly, on this view, the important difference between works of art and other sorts of object must lie in how they appear. Those who hold this view and believe that *Equivalent VIII* is an aesthetically worthless object must contend that this would be so no matter what the history of its production. And those who favour *Equivalent VIII* must also hold that, so far as their aesthetic value is concerned, Andre's bricks, like Ayers Rock, have nothing to do with history. The difference between art and bunk is internal to appearance.

forging ahead

Finally, we saw earlier that those who stress the relevance of intention, context and conditions of production are embarrassed by the pressure this seems to put on the idea that, in the end, what counts, of course, is how the picture or the sculpture looks. For they are committed to holding that though two objects may look the same, yet they may differ in aesthetic value. (If this seems strange now, recall our example of the Moore and the meteorite.) This appears to undercut the centrality of what is seen in what are, after all, the visual arts.

But there is an equal and opposite source of embarrassment on the other side. The problem here centres on the concept of originality. For as this account stands, if we take any work of art that radically changed the possibilities of the medium – consider early Cubist works for example – then we seem forced to conclude that, other things being equal, the clever imitations of the art student will, even if they have no new interest, at least have all the aesthetic interest of the originals.

Since, as it stands, this view allows no reference to the aesthetic significance of the intention with which something was made, we appear forced to absurd conclusions. It will follow, for example, that the artist and forger Tom Keating was the greatest painter of the twentieth century because he could produce objects with the same appearance as those produced by Turner, Cezanne, Matisse, Modigliani *et al*! Either this is so or we are driven to deny, in advance of experience, that such objects could have the same physical appearance as the originals. So it seems that either we are forced to rate the aesthetic worth of the work of talented forgers alongside that of original painters or we are driven to deny that such artful forgery is even possible. And so the embarrassment here is just as acute as that on the other side.

exposing the experts

Despite this, the view that the artist's intentions are irrelevant does enjoy great public popularity. This is because it is often thought to be a neat and effective way of exposing the self-serving and pretentious claims of supposed 'experts' in the art world.

Alternately marvelling and sneering at 'expert opinion' of any kind, especially anything that smacks of intellectualism, is of course a great popular pastime. But there seems a special pleasure to be found in exposing the pretentiousness of experts in the visual arts; one relished by the public and the artist alike. (Commonly, the latter are rather more selective in their damnation.) Now there are no doubt very many complex social and political reasons for this. But there is also a philosophical issue here which needs to be discussed. This issue, concerning what it is to look and to see, is in fact deeply connected with that conception of appearance which leads to the rejection of the relevance of the artist's intention. Let us first see how the view of art under discussion is used to expose the experts.

If we dig beneath the surface of public attitudes towards professionals in the art world, we find that antipathy focuses on what is perceived to be the expert's implicit claim to be a special sort of person. Why are art professionals thought to be making this claim?

It is not that such experts can justly claim to know things that we do not that produces this response. Everyone is quite happy to admit that someone may know more about, say, the history of Renaissance painting or more about the life of Jackson Pollock, or more about the particular circumstances of the creation of Picasso's *Guernica* than either we knew or even knew there was to be known. Such things are, after all, just a matter of knowing *that* such things are or were the case. One doesn't have to be a special sort of person to have such knowledge, we think. One just has to have the time, the opportunity and the desire to acquire such knowledge.

Nor is it that art experts claim to know *how* to do certain things. We are all quite at home with the idea that there are some specialised skills which, through dint of hard work and application, we are capable of acquiring and some in which practice serves only to reveal how hopeless we are and will always remain at this activity. There is no problem here because if we cannot acquire the specialised skill then, for the most part, we are able to avoid and shall certainly not seek out situations which demand its exercise. We do something else instead. So this is not the cause of complaint.

Rather, the source of the popular resentment of 'experts' in the visual arts lies in their implicit claim to be able literally to see things that we do not see. This is why professionals in the visual arts are thought to be claiming to be a special sort of person. The idea that simply seeing may be something that can be developed, refined or improved is one which many people are disposed to find repugnant in the extreme. For, if seeing in this sort of way is a skill, then on the one hand there seems to be no obvious way in which it can be acquired, and on the other, no way of avoiding situations in which its exercise is demanded. If there really is something in, say, the relationships between colours in a painting by Howard Hodgkin, which I cannot see, then who knows what else I am not seeing in the world around me? What, in the landscape or the sunset before me, am I blind to? If I am opposed to the idea of an expert in looking at works of art, it may well be because I think that to accept it is to doom myself to a life as an incompetent looker.

It is just at this point that the line of thought we are discussing is taken to turn the tables on the experts. First of all, in the way it emphasizes the idea of appearance, it lends support to the idea that there cannot be people who are more competent in looking at natural landscapes or at sunsets. It reaffirms that given the same basic capacity, opportunity and interest, all seeing is equal. Secondly, it claims that the aesthetic enjoyment of painting is really no different from that of landscape. So there can no more be real experts in looking at paintings than there can be in looking at sunsets. Insofar as they pretend to be special sorts of person, the experts are exposed.

looking and seeing

The real philosophical interest of all this becomes clear when we reflect that outside of discussions of aesthetics, people will happily agree that, of course, an experienced carpenter can look at a piece of wood and see more than they will and a trained policeman will look at a crowd of hooligans and see the ringleaders far more ably than they ever could. We do not actually think that all seeing is equal. Why this double standard?

What is happening here is that we are being influenced by a particularly powerful philosophical picture of what it is to look at something. We are thinking of looking simply as an attentive kind of seeing. And, rightly or wrongly, we do not think of seeing things as a matter of degree, as a matter of more or less penetration into the visual appearance of things, something in which one might be engaged and at which one might improve. Instead, we think of seeing as all or nothing; as either being visually 'in touch' with the physical surface of objects or not being so. In this sense of 'seeing', though someone of normal vision may try to 'make out' something in the distance, he cannot in normal circumstances 'try' to see what is immediately before his eyes. He opens his eyes and it simply happens. What is seen, the coloured surfaces of things, is simply given to him. Seeing is seeing the surfaces of objects. And the surfaces of objects do not seem to be the sort of thing into which one could more fully delve or about which one might miss something.

If we allow this conception of seeing to dominate our notion of what it is to 'look' at something we arrive at the thought that looking too is a matter of either succeeding or failing to achieve a certain state of affairs. The only difference is that in the case of looking, the achievement is sustained over time. And what we think is given in looking at such surfaces is the visual appearance of the physical properties of objects. This is now taken to be precisely that sense of appearance which is the proper object of aesthetic attention and interest. In this way these conceptions of what it is to look and to see are able to mesh together with what can be considered the central thought of aesthetics, that aesthetic interest is directed towards appearances.

The philosophically interesting source of the popular resentment of art experts, then, is the idea that looking, and hence looking at paintings, is not a skill but an event.

It is, however, an ironic feature of the grip of this idea and its associated notion of appearance on the popular imagination that it has encouraged precisely that kind of work of art which that same public has found so outrageous. In the case of natural objects, the idea of looking as consisting in being directly 'in touch' with the physical properties of objects, leads to the idea that we are properly aesthetically interested only in the physical appearance of natural objects. In the the visual arts, however, it leads to the idea that what can be counted as the appearance of a work of art is just the same sort of thing that can be counted as the appearance of a natural object. It is precisely this, the presentation, say, of pieces of sculpture as being nothing other than physical objects in their own right, in supposed contrast to being aesthetically interesting representations of other objects, that is the central plank in formalist aesthetics. An aesthetics to which works like Andre's scandalizing *Equivalent VIII* give this century's last twists.

rejecting the argument

In assessing the view that artistic intentions are not important, we should be careful not to underestimate the position. In particular, the position should not be rejected because it is thought to be factually incorrect in holding that artists are not discussed or praised or criticised for the work they produce. Or in holding that works of art do not, as a matter of fact, generally look the way that they do because of the character, experience and interests of the artist who made them. Or for holding that it is never illuminating or interesting to know something about the history and context of production of works of art. The argument denies none of this.

What the argument does deny is that such considerations are aesthetic considerations. They happen in our own times to be the surroundings of our aesthetic interest in a particular sort of artefact. But they are not, according to this view, themselves part of the character nor are they among the objects, of aesthetic interest.

Of course, taken in one way, this is not only harmless but perfectly sensible. It is not the case that all our talk about art *must* be aesthetic talk about art. This certainly ought to be remembered more often and we shall have reason to recall it again in the next chapter.

But taken in another way, this line of thought is objectionable because it suggests that considerations about the origin and history of objects can *never* be aesthetic talk about art. If one is to reject the view that artistic intentions are irrelevant, it ought to be because of this thought and its implications. Why?

What the argument achieves is a massive extension in the notion of what can count as a work of art in the visual arts at the price of an equally massive impoverishment of the notion of what can count as an aesthetic property in any of the rest of the arts. As the argument stands, any aesthetically interesting artefact will count as a work of art. But all such objects are deemed to be aesthetically interesting only insofar as their physical appearance is aesthetically interesting. All those properties which contain some implicit reference either to what the artist was thinking and feeling or to the conditions of production of the object will be ruled as illegitimate. Given the richness of the vocabulary of aesthetic concepts we actually employ, this is wantonly destructive. Moreover, it redoubles the difficulties of providing an account of aesthetics that at least has room for *all* the multifarious media of the arts.

The strategy adopted in the argument of this book is precisely opposed to this. We need to restrict the notion of a work of art to a special subset of aesthetically interesting artefacts just in order to allow the widest possible range of types of aesthetic property. In this way, we begin to make room for all the arts.

Hobson's choice

We have seen that we run into different problems when we give different accounts of the relevance of artistic intention to aesthetic interest in works of art. It should now be clear where the source of both sets of problems lies. Both views run into trouble because they tacitly assume that the only proper object of aesthetic attention is the physical appearance of the work of art. Since it is further assumed that the physical appearance of the work, no more than the physical appearance of a meteorite, can support concepts connected with intention, the one view is forced to deny the obvious centrality of appearance, whilst the other is forced to deny the equally obvious relevance of the object's context of production.

What is needed to avoid this Hobson's choice is an account which allows both for the centrality of the appearance of the work and for the fact that the aesthetic value of works of art may be conditioned by their origins. We need to recognise that it can matter, not as a matter of psychology or sociology but *aesthetically* when, where, by whom and why a work of art was produced. And we need to recognise that this is consistent with the central idea in aesthetics – that aesthetic interest is directed towards appearances, with how things seem, with the fact that there is a sense in which how things things really are does not matter in aesthetics. It is here that the concept of the intended appearance of the work comes to the fore.

irrelevant or redundant?

Before returning to this central idea we must examine another line of thought which also arrives at the conclusion that the difference between art and bunk is to be found in the appearance of the object and not in what the artist's intentions were in producing such an object. But it must be described separately because it arrives at this conclusion by a rather different route. To be sure, it does also seek to direct our attention away from allegedly irrelevant considerations concerning the origins of the object to the 'genuinely aesthetic' interest in the appearance of the object. But it tries to do this without relying on the thought that appearances which are the proper objects of aesthetic interest must be physical appearances, describable only in terms which would apply also to natural objects.

On the contrary, on this view, the relevant appearance of

the object may be shot through with concepts which it would be absurd to apply to natural objects: all the sorts of concepts which it seemed possible to apply to the Henry Moore piece but not on any account to the physically identical meteorite.

Now, given the origins of this argument, the insistence that not all aesthetic properties must be physical properties ought to come as no surprise. For this attack on what the proponents of the argument characterised as the 'intentional fallacy' had its primary application in the context of works of literature. And in the aesthetics of literature, there is simply not the same danger, as there is in the case of the visual arts, of seeking to assimilate works of art to aesthetically arresting natural objects.

The argument proceeds not by reference to what may be a proper object of aesthetic attention but rather by reference to what is relevant to the understanding of that object of attention, whatever it might be.

The argument is directed against a range of theories of art, which can be called 'intentionalist theories'. What these theories are alleged to have in common is that they presuppose or imply the claim that in coming to understand or judge a work of art – in our stark terms, deciding whether or not something is art or bunk – it is legitimate and relevant to refer to the independently describable intentions of the artist. That is, intentions describable independently of the work. This, of course, is precisely the sort of claim mentioned earlier – that in order to judge the worth of *Equivalent VIII* we might first have to listen to what Andre has to say.

While it has never been easy to specify exactly what is supposed to be fallacious in the alleged intentional fallacy, the basic thrust of the argument which exposes it is this. In regard to a particular work, either the artist successfully carried out her intentions in making that work or she failed to carry out her intentions. If she succeeded, then what she intended to do is already perceivable in the work of art. Talk about her intentions which is not talk about the work is redundant. If she failed, then what she intended is not perceivable in the work. But then talk about her intentions is irrelevant. So there cannot be independent descriptions of artistic intentions which are both relevant and non-redundant. Since this is just what intentionalist theories claim, they must all be false.

A typical application of this argument would be this. A scholar might claim that *The Tempest* is an allegory of the life of a dramatist because he has discovered a letter from Shakespeare announcing that he will write just such a play, and will call it 'The Tempest'. Now either Shakespeare carried out his intention or, for whatever reason, he didn't. If he did, then we have no need of the letter. For the allegory will be apparent in the play. If he did not, then *The Tempest* isn't such an allegory and the letter is irrelevant.

Now, while this argument was largely developed in terms of literature – indeed it became one of the central dogmas of the so-called 'New Criticism' that had developed into a critical orthodoxy by the middle of this century – if correct, it applies to all the media of art.

For a perfectly possible, if less typical application, is this. A critic may claim that Andre's *Equivalent VIII* is bunk because nothing that Andre has said about his intentions in producing it makes any sense at all. Now either this nonsense is reflected in what Andre produces or it is not. If it is, then *Equivalent VIII* will make no more sense than Andre's descriptions or justifications of it. But then we do not need to listen to Andre to know this. If it is not, then Andre is a better artist than a talker. And so what he says should be ignored. So again, reference to what the artist intended or says or thinks or feels is either irrelevant or redundant. Hence the difference between art and bunk must consist in the available appearance of the object.

It is important to stress that the central claim of this argument is not, as before, that the artist's intentions are never relevant because they can never be part of the appearance of the object. For it is proposed here that we can see what an artist intended by attending to the appearance of the objects he produces. The claim is that all that is relevant to understanding and making judgements about the aesthetic interest of the object is the appearance of the object. On this view, it is because intention can be manifest in the appearance of a work of art that there is never any need to go outside the work. Works of art are not to be assimilated to natural objects. But, like natural objects, they are autonomous.

rejecting the argument

This attack on intentionalist aesthetics certainly represents a step forward from the earlier attack on the place of intention in art. In its economy and clarity, it has seemed to many an attractive argument.

But while it rejects the identification of relevant aesthetic appearance with physical appearance, it still shares with the earlier account an important assumption about the appearance of paintings, sculpture, and also novels, poems and so on. The assumption is that what counts as the appearance of the object in each case is something that can be thought of as given independently of an audience's capacity to apprehend it. The argument works only because 'what is perceivable in a work' and so what can be said to be 'embodied in a work' are thought of as constants against which the relevance of 'external' information can be tested. And this can be so only if we already exclude knowledge of such information from being an element in the competence which an audience brings to a work.

But this is to completely misdescribe the phenomenon under scrutiny. Indeed, it gets things exactly backwards. It is as if we were to think of a criminal trial as a process whereby the accused is presumed to be innocent in order to try potentially perjurious witnesses. For in seeking to understand, say, the iconography of *Guernica,* we are not in the business of assessing whether or not the information we happen to have acquired about Basque churches may be legitimately included as evidence for what we find we have to say. What we find we have to say has yet to be determined. This is because what we may take to be the appearance of the painting has yet to be determined. When this begins to be determined it will in part be because of what, if anything, the information we have acquired enables us to see.

Thus it may be that what we know about Basque churches does not enable us to see anything in *Guernica* that we could not see already: any member of our culture may be justly presumed to be able to recognise the theme of Calvary. On the other hand, it may transform everything: only in the light of our acquaintance with a particular set of Basque religious paintings is it possible to discern the additional level of structure imposed upon the painting. And this affects what we now see in some other aspect of the work. It now becomes possible to see why some aspect or portion of the painting appears as it does. Relative to this background, the appearance of the painting becomes intelligible.

Consider also when we are aware of other works an artist has produced. Nothing in *Four Quartets* announces that its author was also the writer of *The Wasteland*. But how much does someone unfamiliar with the earlier work miss in the later? What can be said to be apparent in *Four Quartets* is something relative to a background of competence in a reader. The poems are not prefaced with a precise description of the competence required. But they assume that the need for some capacities and background information will be recognised as a just demand on an audience. Indeed, it is just because of this that *The Wasteland*, with its ponderously scholastic footnotes, is able to raise the question of the extent to which its audience still shares a common fund of values and meanings against the background of which the poem can be read.

That what we are able to see in a painting is in part determined by what we are able to bring to bear on it does not mean that there is no limit at all on what might be thought to be relevant to the understanding of a work. This would mean that the work of art has no appearance which is independent of how it is seen by particular individuals. But because we cannot determine in advance what limits there are on the relevance of the background competence we bring to bear does not mean that, in practice, we shall not encounter limits. To know that Andre once worked on the Pennsylvania Railway, moving largely identical cars from one place to another, is one thing. To know that he admires the paintings of Edward Hopper, quite another. Armed with the first piece of information, one may begin to discern in *Equivalent VIII* a disturbing obsession with order for its own sake. That the bricks have been arranged in that way begins to be intelligible in the light of this thought. By contrast, the second piece of information seems to take us nowhere.

What in fact the limits to such competence are in the case of a particular work is something to be discovered in the course of exploring the work. What is needed cannot be decided in advance. But this does not mean that everything is needed in advance.

So, against the attractive economy of the anti-intentionalist argument must be set the need to recognise that the important question is not whether the information and knowledge we bring to bear on the painting is relevant because legitimately acquired, but whether it is relevant because it affects the intelligibility of what can be seen. Just as no one should predict in advance whether a jury will place its faith in the testimony of the accused or in that of the witnesses, so we cannot determine in advance what sort of information might or might not illuminate some feature of a work of art. That is something to be found only as we proceed in our explorations. No one can decide in advance what sorts of knowledge, what sorts of given or acquired competence in the audience, will produce a differ-ence in what we take the appearance of the painting to consist. Properly understood, this is to insist even more forcefully than the anti-intentionalist argument on the centrality of appearance in art.

how to fail as an artist
The thought that relevant information about the artist's inten-tions affects what we find to be the appearance of his work gives us a useful grip on different kinds of artistic failure; on sorts of difference between art and bunk. This is because to know more about what an artist intended need not necessarily heighten or enhance the intelligibility of what is seen. On the contrary, there are a number of ways in which intelligibility can diminish as a result of relevant information about the origins of a work.

First of all, coming to acquire relevant information may

throw us into confusion. Given what we now know we can no longer make sense of what we see: we feel that we have to learn to see with fresh eyes. If our knowledge of the plays makes a difference to what we are able to find in Shakespearean sonnets, then it is simply dishonest to claim that it does not matter if the plays were in fact written by Bacon.

Secondly, to come to know more about what an artist intended may enable us to see that he does not know what he is doing in the work before us. His work seemed to us to be serious or witty, moving or technically innovative but this was an illusion. We now think less of it as a work of art.

Thirdly, and most serious of all, the work may become less intelligible in that it ceases to make sense to regard it as a work of art. These are ways in which an artist may have failed to produce a work of art; ways in which an artist may run the risk of producing bunk.

First of all, we may discover that the sort of knowledge an artist demands of her audience is inconsistent with seeing what she has produced as a work of art.

The reason for this is that we must over the long run be able to distinguish between what it makes sense to say can be seen in the appearance of the work and what must be said to be only idiosyncratically associated with the object.

Consider the point first of all from the position of a member of an audience. It may be that whenever I see a particular painting by Rothko, I cannot help smiling nostalgically to myself. The hue of that central slab of colour is precisely the hue of a old jumper of which I was once so fond.

Now it is true to say that I am smiling because of the colour of the object made by Rothko. The physical object hanging on the wall has the colour of my jumper and so has the power to make me have such thoughts.

But it would not make sense to say that, because of this, the painting can be described as nostalgic or fond. This is because we are not interested in all the causal properties of the object. We are aesthetically interested in how the way the work looks is related to why it looks as it does. How these interpenetrate. And this means that very many of the object's causal properties are simply not relevant. So even though the object causes me to have certain nostalgic thoughts, this need not be any part of what it can make sense to say is seen in the painting. The relation between how the work looks and what someone sees is not a question of the existence or non-existence of a causal connection. It is a question of success or failure in understanding.

So, even though I am smiling because of the object made by Rothko, I am not smiling because of the painting. I am only smiling in the company of the painting.

Now note that precisely the same is true if it is Rothko who is prone to such associations. Nor does anything change if the associations are with more interesting and more profound emotions than those engendered by memories of a favourite jumper.

This puts a formal limit on the sorts of background knowledge that an artist may hold to be relevant to a work. For how we acquire that information and what we are able to do with it must be consistent with regarding the object as a work of art. If the information we need is simply that the artist has, at some time in the past, made a set of private one-to-one associations, say between certain sorts of feeling and particular colours, and all the properties of the work are only explicable through reference to this fact, then we are dealing not with a kind of work of art but with a kind of *code*. Such a work is only *incidentally* coloured. Its being coloured in that way is not an essential part of how it looks. All that is essential to how the work looks is that the object has some elements or other that can have these quasi-semantic connections.

It may be that some of these collections of signs going proxy for meanings will be prettier than others. Some may be genuinely aesthetically interesting. But they will be so only in the way that a natural object or a simple artefact might. The patterns made by laying out seashells on the beach in braille may be very beautiful. And one may say beautiful things in braille. But there is no essential relation between these things. If it happens that saying something interesting produces an interesting pattern, this is only a happy coincidence.

Compare the human voice. It is not a happy coincidence that to speak gently is part of speaking gentle things.

So if what an artist produces is intelligible only if regarded as something which physically represents a code, then there is no aesthetic difference between making such an object according to a previously conceived set of correspondences and choosing such correspondences to match the salient features of a previously existing natural object. An object made by an artist in this way might therefore just as well be a natural object.

An object which fails to be a work of art in this way may still, like a newly decorated room, be genuinely aesthetically interesting. It may indeed be aesthetically interesting to relate the aesthetic properties of the object to the features of other objects, whether natural or made. Indeed, Andre claimed that it was his pleasure in finding a brick in the street, a beautiful white brick made of synthetic limestone, that, together with his experience of rowing across a calm lake, made him begin to contemplate making the *Equivalent* series.

Where there is enough agreement about the interest of such an object, it may become natural to compare its properties with properties that may belong to some works of art. Thus we might fruitfully compare the flatness of *Equivalent VIII* with the extent to which painters in this century have sought to use physical flatness on canvasses to imitate or allude to the non-three-dimensionality of the paintings they produce. Note that such comparisons might be equally legitimate if it were agreed on all sides that *Equivalent VIII* was not a work of art. In this way, then, something that is not a work of art can come to occupy a place in the history of works of art. There is nothing strange about this. Too often we get into tangles about what is and what isn't a work of art simply because we think that any middle-sized aesthetically interesting object that occupies a place of importance in the history of art must therefore be a work of art.

In this way an artist may produce an object that not only is aesthetically interesting; that not only may be interestingly compared with works of art but which may also come to have a place in the history of art. And it may have been that the artist intended that all this was to happen. And yet it may still not make sense for us to call this object a work of art. This is just a consequence of the view that, if the notion of a work of art is to play any role in aesthetic experience, then there must be a difference between works of art and merely aesthetically interesting objects.

how to be a bigger failure

There is another, deeper kind of failure which is also possible. For in attempting to produce a work of art, an artist may produce an object that is aesthetically interesting only to a particular person, under certain, perhaps very transient, conditions. In this case we cannot attend aesthetically to the *intended* appearance of such an object because, if the relevant appearance of the work just is how it appears to a particular individual, perhaps the artist, under particular conditions, perhaps on a Sunday morning, seen through the mist coming up the river, then the object cannot be said to have such an appearance. It does not have an intended appearance which is not available to anyone else.

There is a third and still more profound way in which an artist might fail to make a work of art. An artist may produce an object which is aesthetically interesting only in the grip of the attitude or frame of mind, mentioned in the previous chapter, in which we find ourselves somehow attuned to the specialness or the sacredness of the ordinary and common-place. In such a frame of mind we can find ourselves attending aesthetically to the 'particularity' of an object in such a way that, to put the feeling at its most baldly paradoxical, we feel that every object is unique.

For some, this feeling of the uniqueness of the familiar constitutes a too rare realisation that the real (and for the poet and priest Gerard Manley Hopkins as for others, the divine) is given in the particularity of the commonplace. Indeed, for many such thinkers the value of art lies precisely in its power to redirect our attention to the holy which, on this view, can *only* lie in what is always close at hand.

But though there may be connections between this sense

of 'particularity' and that pervasive sense of 'fit' mentioned earlier, the extent to which an artist presents us with objects which can be found aesthetically interesting solely through such a state of mind is the extent to which he fails to produce objects which it makes sense to call works of art. This must be accepted even by those who hold this state of mind to be at the heart of artistic endeavour. For this purpose is not achieved merely by the provision of a stream of *examples* of the commonplace and the familiar. Hopkins did not worship the divinity in the ordinary by writing ordinary verse. He wrestled with language until its words sparked and the ordinary could be newly seen by their light.

These are some ways in which an artist, though perhaps intending to make a work of art and though, at best, succeeding in making an aesthetically interesting object that has a place alongside works of art, may yet fail to produce anything which it makes sense to think of as art.

We can now see at least one source of the bunk that characterises so much of the theory and practice of the tradition of the visual arts in this century.

The concept of art tells us to expect aesthetically intelligible objects, objects whose intended appearance rewards perceptual exploration. In the case of the artefacts we have been discussing we know both that the objects have aesthetic interest and that they were made with this in mind. But in trying to make these two ideas mesh *in what we can see*, in trying to find the objects intelligible, we run the risk of generating the nonsense we would produce if asked to explain why, *aesthetically*, a tree or a landscape looks as it does. What is there to talk but nonsense?

summary

Where does this leave the claim that the difference between art and bunk should be understood in terms of what lies behind the work? What must we say about this claim that a work of art should be thought of as an aesthetically interesting artefact which has been produced as the result of relevant and appropriate intentions?

The two arguments we have examined against this position strike telling blows. Together they draw our attention to the fact that any account which pushes the appearance of a work from centre stage fails to do justice to the nature of aesthetic interest. The present appearance is the appropriate object of aesthetic attention. We cannot buy the relevance of the origins of the object in the artist by selling off how the object appears. But we do not need to. What we should do is to reflect on what the impossibility of choosing between these alternatives teaches us. We should recognise that both views capture important aspects of our experience of works of art, and we should seek instead to reconcile them.

We reconcile them first by holding that, of course, the appearance must be central but what counts as the relevant appearance here is the appearance of the work. Not the appearance of the paint on the canvas, not the wood, and not the physical movement, but the canvas as painted, the wood as carved, the movement as danced. There is nothing difficult about applying concepts involving reference to the origins of the object to these appearances. To attend to the appearance of the carved wood is already to be aware of something of the origins of that appearance. This possibility is built into that of seeing it as carved. We reconcile the centrality of appearance with the importance of the fact that works of art have been made by someone, by insisting on the conclusion to the preceding chapter: in the case of works of art the relevant appearance is the intended appearance of the object.

But in resisting the pull of the anti-intentionalist argument, we saw that this alone is not enough. For we need to hold that what counts as the intended appearance, the work, is not something fixed to the object, as a canvas is to a frame. Rather we need the idea that what counts as the intended appearance is something relative to a background of competence on the part of an audience. This is an idea that we take with us into the next chapter.

notes

p.37. The distinction between natural and non-natural meaning was originally drawn by H.P. Grice in 'Meaning', *Philosophical Review* Vol. 66 (1957) pp.377-88, reprinted in *Philosophical Logic* ed. P.F. Strawson, (Oxford, Oxford University Press, 1967).

p.38. For a lucid account of the importance of distinctions between reasons and causes for aesthetics see 'Art History and Aesthetic Judgement' in *The Aesthetic Understanding*, Roger Scruton, (London, Methuen & Co. Ltd, 1983) especially pp. 170-1.

p.49. The notion of the 'intentional fallacy' was originally developed by W.K. Wimsatt and M. Beardsley in 'The Intentional Fallacy', c.f. *The Verbal Icon*, W.K. Wimsatt, (Lexington, University of Kentucky Press, 1954).

p.55. Paintings may have many causal properties which are irrelevant to our aesthetic interest in the works even if we cannot miss noticing such properties. A Canadian company, Global Star Products Ltd., markets Artwarmers™: 'original works of art' which can be plugged into the mains and which then radiate infra-red heat into the room. The publicity material for 'Radiant Art' is to be praised for carefully distinguishing the aesthetically relevant aspects of Artwarmers from their other properties: 'It's an original work of art! It's a safe, efficient room heater!' Thus one might say of such a work: 'It's a rotten painting but at least it's *warm*.'

p.58. The poems of Hopkins are in *Gerard Manley Hopkins – Poems and Prose,* selected and edited by W.H. Gardener (Harmondsworth, Penguin, 1953).

3: art and the audience

Is the sort of difference there is between art and bunk a sort of difference which is independent of what individuals think is art and what they think is bunk? Or must what we judge and what we do not judge to be works of art depend upon who and what we are? Is it really possible to *know* that something is aesthetically valuable? Is the aesthetic value of something just a matter of personal judgement? Can any of this be a matter of 'right' and 'wrong'? To reverse the popular saying: when it comes to art, isn't bunk in the eye of the beholder?

In this chapter we shall try to understand these questions correctly. We shall see that they attempt to capture very important features of our experience of works of art but that they do so in terms of a set of distorted pictures of the relevant concepts and capacities. So what we shall try to do here is to disentangle what is true and harmless from what is false and misleading.

a nightwatchman discipline
First of all, why is it important to understand these questions correctly? Many people have thought these questions important because they have believed that if they are dealt with properly there will be no need to consider further issues concerning art and aesthetic experience. For having answered the prior questions, we shall see that the philosophical consideration of these further matters is essentially pointless.

What groups of people have held this view? Many philosophers have certainly argued this, though they have tended to be philosophers whose prime concerns lie outside aesthetics and who wish to use the philosophy of art as a test bed for arguments and principles of more general philosophical interest. Many artists often appear to think just this, although those that really do often have difficulty reconciling the view with their practice. Certainly this opinion is ever present in many public discussions that verge on questions of art and aesthetics.

Indeed, just about the only groups of people who do not generally share this view and have found other aspects of aesthetic phenomena more fruitful to reflect upon, have been professional art critics and professional philosophers of art. But then, they would, wouldn't they?

This seems a just riposte because the relevant thought is something like this. Reflection upon aesthetic phenomena, including the facts of how people behave in this sphere, teaches us that aesthetic phenomena are not objects of public knowledge but objects of personal experience. This explains why there exists massive disagreement about aesthetic phenomena. If we take only the case of works of art, not only do people everywhere make different judgements about different works and artists, styles and genres, periods and media, they cannot now even agree about what is and what isn't a work of art at all. Witness our ubiquitous *Equivalent VIII*. And all this disagreement within a single culture!

Therefore, all that critics in the arts can do is to inform us of their personal judgements which, though they may be more articulately expressed than those of the average member of an audience, should in the end carry no more weight. For in fact all such judgements are, as it were, equally weightless.

But if this is true, then it has implications for the philosophy of art. It becomes pointless to seek to clarify, say, the concept of art. For there is no agreed concept. Or at least, there is no agreement about its application, which is to say that there is a question mark over the existence of this concept. It is therefore pointless to produce philosophical theories about aesthetic phenomena. All that philosophical inquiry into aesthetics ought to do is to state and restate this truth about the relativity of aesthetic phenomena and expose the fallacies in the arguments of those who suggest otherwise. The field can then be reserved for those disciplines which take objects of personal experience as their proper objects. Thus psychology may investigate, say, the mechanics of mind that enter into our perception of aesthetic properties and the social sciences may investigate, say, how it is that individual judgements are transmitted across a culture and through time.

Such work may be both interesting and fruitful. But philosophical aesthetics ought itself to be only a kind of nightwatchman discipline. It may be that individuals can use aesthetics to gain currency for new sets of ideas in the arts and to further increase the diversity of objects of aesthetic interest. It may be natural for those engaged in this discipline, like art critics themselves, to think they are doing more than defending sets of personal preferences. But they should be mindful that the real task of the philosophy of art is only to keep out intruders that others might be left secure and undisturbed to get on with their work.

There is therefore, on this view, no general answer to the question of the sort of difference there is between art and bunk. Or if there is, it is only that it belongs to the nature of art that there are as many lines between these two things as there are people willing to draw them and even then they are always drawn in pencil and never in ink.

So, despite the progress we appeared to have been making in the last two chapters in delineating the sort of contrast there is between art and bunk, there may in fact be no such contrast at all. This is why it is important to understand these questions correctly.

Let us try to discover just what the source of this set of questions is. What exactly is it that we are trying to say when we claim that there can be no general solutions to problems in aesthetics; that these are matters of judgement, preference or opinion? Or that there is no disputing about taste? That these are not matters of knowledge? That *subjectivity* is at the centre of things in this sphere?

There does indeed seem to be something important that people want to say by using such terms and by making such remarks. The fact that such people use such different formulations suggests that the situation people want to describe demands that they say something without making it clear exactly what this should be. Let us proceed by elimination and get clear about what the problem cannot be.

nobody knows anything?

Is the source of the problem this? Do we mean that human beings never in fact know anything – that everywhere we think there is knowledge, there is really only belief and opinion and personal judgement? So that what I can say is always limited only to how things seem to me. And since this is as true of works of art as of anything else, this is why we want to say that our experience of works of art is personal and not a matter of knowledge.

There is of course a long tradition of such scepticism about the possibility of knowledge, any knowledge, in philosophy. And though it is often claimed that such scepticism is empty or inexpressible or self-refuting, it may well be that this is a ghost which neither can be nor ought to be laid to rest. Indeed, the fact that scepticism about the possibility of any knowledge can keep coming back to haunt us in so many different guises may be telling us something important about the nature of human knowledge. Like any other intellectual tradition, these thoughts have fed into the history of art, art criticism and aesthetics in our century. And, in particular, when the world has been so dangerous a place that the practice of art has seemed to artists a kind of refuge, they have often erected the defensive barrier of such scepticism around their work. The hope is that scepticism will provide a proper foundation for tolerance. It is in part because of this that younger artists often appear to find this general position attractive.

But it cannot be this general scepticism about the possibility of knowledge which we are concerned with here. It may be natural to retreat to this position when under threat, but it cannot really be this that we mean to say when we talk about subjectivity in our experience of works of art. For this general scepticism applies to everything: from aesthetics, to physics, to what we gave the cat for dinner. But, if we really mean to say something about our experience of works of art, we must leave something in the world with which to contrast this experience. If it is important to say that aesthetic experience is not a matter of knowledge, then some things must be. So, what we have to say must mean something more specific to aesthetic experience than such generalised scepticism will allow.

People have widely different sets of aesthetic preferences.

diversity of interest?

If what we have to say is something far more specific to the particular circumstances in which we encounter works of art, isn't the relevant fact this? Don't different people tend to think and say different things whilst looking at the same work of art?

The proper response to this thought is to agree. For example, you might be interested in a painting because it depicts a place you once visited, and I am interested in it because I think I would like to own it and I'm trying to get my wife to agree to buy it. You say things like 'Ah – St André de Valborgne – *so* peaceful!' And I say things like 'It would look wonderful on that wall, don't you think so? And it really is a good investment'. Of course we will say different things: we have different interests: yours nostalgic, mine acquisitive. And of course there are all sorts of other interests we might have – other than aesthetic interests – which would lead us to think and say different things.

This is only at all problematic if we have managed to convince ourselves that everything we think or feel or say whilst in the company of works of art ought really to be aesthetically relevant thoughts, feelings and talk. But this is quite impossibly pompous. It gives to our interest in works of art a semi-religious, ritual character – the art gallery as cathedral where everything we do either is or should be part of the sacred ceremony – that is both absurd and dangerous.

So, that people say and think different things when looking at works of art cannot be the source of the problem.

diversity of aesthetic interest?

Is this the problem? When people are pursuing aesthetic interests, don't people come to like and dislike different things? Don't people have widely different sets of aesthetic preferences? Some people devote their lives to following opera. Others enjoy only small, still pieces of ceramic. Some people are mad to hear avant-garde music. Others will do almost anything to avoid it. There are those who find contemporary arts to be amongst the most important things in their lives. And there are also those, the vast majority, who, while they are constantly making all the aesthetic adjustments and decisions that permeate ordinary life, have no interest whatsoever in such matters.

If all this is as described, doesn't this show that it is futile to seek knowledge and agreement on the sort of difference there is between art and bunk and hence to seek to know what sort of thing a work of art is?

Not at all, certainly not as described. Whatever it is we really want to say is here colouring our perception of perfectly ordinary facts. And in the process it is also distorting the very important idea of preference. We shall return to this later. For the present we should only note the idea that lies behind the insistence that there is here an insurmountable problem for aesthetics.

First of all, notice that no one draws such conclusions in other fields. The world is full of schoolchildren who prefer, say, biology to physics. And there must be biologists who find zoology to be tedious by comparison with molecular genetics. And the vast majority of people neither know nor care much about either. But it would be absurd to conclude that because such preferences exist, there is nothing we can fruitfully say about physics or biology and its sub-disciplines; that the differences between these things are themselves a matter of preference.

This is not to say that the arts are like scientific disciplines. But only to make the quite general point that it is fallacious to argue that because we have different preferences in respect of something, it follows that personal preference is central to the character of that thing. Equally of course, we might have reasons for doing something which everyone agrees to – it hardly follows that what we all agree to do is itself free from all matters of personal preference. There might be reasons we could all agree upon as to why someone should become a gourmet or a wine-connoisseur.

One reason why we forget such truths is that we get entranced by the pictures embedded in that endlessly ambiguous term 'subjectivity'. This is a term with an incredibly complex history; a philosophical football that has been kicked around so much that no one has any idea who really owns it or what game to play with it. Consequently, we cannot today use this term and its correlates without seeming to commit ourselves to the truth of a whole assortment of dogmas and dictums. Principal amongst these is the view that whatever is a matter of experience cannot also be a matter of knowledge.

This is a widely-held view, but on reflection it is clear that it conflates two different ideas. It is one idea for something to belong essentially to experience, to be bound up within the experiences of people, subjects, considered quite generally. But it is quite another for judgements about or connected with this thing to have no reach beyond some particular subject – to be 'true' only for some particular individual; for me or you or Bloggs; to be therefore not a matter of knowledge.

Consider an example. Colour is perhaps properly called 'subjective' in the first sense. It is not something it makes sense to talk about independently of the possibility of there being subjects capable of experiencing it. But it hardly follows that what I say about colour is 'subjective' in the second sense. So that I can never be said to *know* that British pillar boxes are red.

Moreover, even if this did follow, it would not in turn entail that I only *believe* them to be red. As if pillar boxes might all along be blue or green and no one knew! For this then creates the impression that there is something right in front of our noses which lies forever beyond the bounds of human knowledge.

Tracing all the origins of this confused notion of subjectivity is too large a philosophical task to undertake here. The point for the moment is that it is only against the background of such confusions that, on its own, the claim that people have preferences in the arts can be thought to be the source of the supposed problem. That there is something especially problematic about the idea of knowledge in connection with aesthetics cannot hinge simply on the diversity of aesthetic interest.

diversity within aesthetic interest?
So is the problem this? Don't different people tend to think and say different things even where they make similar judgements and have similar preferences, and where they are pursuing or

expressing their aesthetic interest in the same work of art?

But again we should agree with this. It is an important fact. But not for the reason supposed here. For the sake of familiarity, consider again *Guernica*. Now it may well be that whilst you and I, who both greatly admire this work, are looking at the painting, you find yourself becoming increasingly intrigued by its depiction of the horror of war. Perhaps you begin to wonder if the Calvary theme, so pervasive in the painting, is not at odds with the central image of the suffering horse – Christ's crucifixion was hardly a pointless or futile sacrifice and yet the suffering of animals, most especially in war, seems precisely that. How does the theme of valuable death apply to the Nazi raid on *Guernica*? Is there a lacuna in Picasso's vision here or is this part of the painting's concerns?

As you pursue and express such thoughts, I am occupied with different matters. What I find difficult in this painting is to understand whether its form, with its splintered spaces, is meant to embody chaos and disorder, or whether the form forces us to seek a unifying order in the picture. Different aspects of the painting point in different ways. And so on.

Now the careful consideration of such diverse chains of thought is indeed philosophically enlightening. We learn something about the sorts of aesthetic concepts that we use and the different levels on which we use them. But there is nothing here so problematic as to force us to say that if this is what talk about art is like, then further reflection is pointless. For perhaps what each of us says here complements what the other has to say. The things we find problematic or difficult to understand are all aspects of the painting.

incompatible interests?
But if this is not the source of the problem either, perhaps we are getting closer. For is it not that people say *incompatible* things about works of art?

Certainly people do this. And that they can say incompatible things is extremely interesting. For first of all, if what they say really is incompatible, then this means that they are doing something other than expressing their personal preferences. To avow my personal preference is not to say anything which could, in this sense, be incompatible with your avowal of your preference. It is, after all, only rarely, with people we know well, that we do dispute whether someone has correctly or sincerely avowed their own real preference: 'Surely you don't like *that*! Not you of all people.'

Second, this is not the only relevant sense of incompatibility. What I say may be incompatible with what you say. But what *I* say may also be incompatible with *your* saying what you do. This is connected with the importance of the idea of preference, and we should break off here to say something about it. We will then return to the question of the incompatibility of what we each say.

preference and principle

It is necessary to think about preference and incompatibility because too often statements of the problem that we are trying to describe here trade on a false contrast between high cognition and brute preference.

The contrast is this. Our aesthetic interest issues in *mere* preference; what we say is *only* a matter of taste. Why? Because we think we must picture justifiable beliefs as steel girders; the superscaffolding that binds thought into the edifice of knowledge. Justified beliefs matter.

Preferences and tastes, on the other hand, must be pictured as atoms of hurrahs and boos that whiz and swerve to little consequence. And this may be why we think we should be tolerant of people's tastes and preferences. First, because they are not really under their control. And second, because they do not really matter.

Coming to understand correctly the sorts of relations there are between an audience and works of art is a matter both of softening and dissolving what is in this picture of cognition, and of binding and unifying what we find in our picture of preference. It is a matter of coming to see that if we are tolerant of people's tastes and preferences, it is not because they do not really matter but because tastes and preferences may run deep inside a person. They are therefore deserving of the sort of respect which we accord to persons.

To do what we can to break the grip of these pictures, consider how preferences can be incompatible. First of all, many of the matters about which we have preferences are not trivial. Matters of taste often do run very deep; they may indeed be profoundly important to us. Consider the role played by taste and preference in people's religious lives – imagine someone saying 'Which bible we use doesn't matter – it's *only* a matter of taste.' Yet clearly it may be a matter of taste. It's just that people can be prepared to live and die for their preferences as well as for their principles. Their preferences can be matters of principle. Which is not to say that they are principles disguised as preferences.

Secondly, it is a fact about us that we want our preferences to relate to each other in structured ways. Such sets of tastes and preferences give unity and security to our lives. This is true even of the most catholic of us. We think of sets of preferences and tastes as ways of being someone. We know that the more we acquire and cultivate such preferences, the more deeply they both reflect and shape our characters. We might also think here of what we mean by someone's style. Not in the sense in which we say that someone has style, though this is related. But in the sense in which we talk of the style of a man's or woman's life, something that permeates everything they do. In this sense style is deeply implicated in what we understand by the notions of integrity and character: it is a kind of unity to the myriad aspects of one's life that goes beyond consistency or sameness.

And in making sense of such unifying features, our aesthetic preferences are particularly important. At their most general, they awaken us to possibilities of structure and order, of 'fittedness' between perhaps very different kinds of entity and quality, that weave our lives together. Such a sense of fit is deeply implicated in our ethical sense. The ancient idea that the unjust or the wicked put the balance of things out of kilter is not just a metaphor. It appeals to deeply built-in preferences for symmetries over the large scale.

But we are not limited to finding satisfactions simply in balances of mass. There are very different kinds of order. To be struck, for example, by the mix and match between the ambitions of youth and the achievements of middle age is to be struck by more subtle patterns of order and chaos – their appreciation may well demand an essentially aesthetic sensibility! Again, to be capable of finding comfort in the ironies that pepper our disasters is possible only against the background of sensitivity to something which is sometimes a kind of incongruity in order, and at other times, a kind of order in incongruity.

Such possibilities are intrinsic to the values of the arts. It is another order of this kind that a painter may explore through different colours or in making colour live with space and shape. And such a painting can make us alive to new possibilities of order and relation. This is why when we see a really fine abstract painting, of whatever modernist school, to call it abstract does not seem in any way a relevant thing to say about it. One feels that one might as well say that the sad or the tragic is an abstract feature of certain situations. And then when we see paintings that do nothing but advertise their subject as paint on flat canvas, we are terribly disappointed. We feel like saying 'Yes – of course you should be concerned with colour and paint and the flat surface of the canvas. But not in that way! Ask yourself why these things matter.'

And this ought to be familiar. It is in part the enhancement of just such sensitivities to the affective character of sorts of order and disorder that we understand by the education of the sentiments, so long an acknowledged function of music and literature, painting and drama. And we do well to recognise that the sentiments in need of education are not limited to the pious and the effete. The affective implications of patterns of order and relation cover the whole range of human capacities.

On the one hand the capacity to laugh out loud at ourselves, for our pomposity or pretension, is something unimaginable in a kind of being that was not capable of enjoying complex kinds of order. The funny is a categorically aesthetic mode of apprehending the world.

On the other hand, the role that such sensibilities can play in our lives can engender very different capacities. It is only via people's essentially aesthetic ways of understanding the world that some recent architecture has been able to reach in, immure and brutalise the spirit of those who must live with it every day.

It is because our preferences, especially our aesthetic preferences, can shape us and our lives in such ways that different kinds of incompatibility between preferences become possible. It is because of such things perhaps that, for your sake, you should like my tastes to run with yours. That they do not, or do not any more, means that *we* are incompatible or that those parts of our lives are. The domains in which friendships may safely operate can be determined by patterns of compatible and incompatible preferences. Sharing a sense of humour, so often cited as a foundation for relationships, is the overlapping of modes of aesthetic attention. And the sorts of order that preferences can reach out to may not be apparent. Think how shocked we can be when we find ourselves or others laughing at that poor joke, or his misfortune, or that grotesque thought.

Again, perhaps my having those preferences, being upset by that sort of thing, is incompatible with who it is you wanted me to be. Or perhaps your dislike for it or him is a betrayal of me. And now perhaps the light this lends to what you say makes me think that, even where you agreed with me, we were really saying different things. These are the kinds of incompatibility and contradiction which play prominent roles in people's lives. They are part and parcel of having preferences and tastes.

This is important. It reminds us that preferences and tastes are not just shadows cast by beliefs, stretching and shrinking without consequence. They are themselves sources of illumination.

And so we should beware when we hear talk of mere preferences and something being only a matter of taste. For this runs the risk of distorting both the character of aesthetic experience and the sorts of sense which it is possible to make out of our lives.

incompatible judgements?
To return to our process of elimination, is the problem that makes it impossible to say something substantial about the

difference between art and bunk, really that *what* people think and say about works of art may be incompatible? You complain that Bosch is unintelligible – the images have a significance that is now lost to us. But my view is that everything in the nightmares of his work is clear. Just as clear as it is supposed to be. So according to us the paintings are both unintelligible and perfectly intelligible.

Again, we must mean something more than this. For this sort of disagreement is something common to very many human activities: of course people disagree.

But in these other areas, the disputes are resolved. Evidence is brought to bear, beliefs are tested, conclusions reached.

So too in our dealings with each other over works of art. It is not as if people never reach agreement over anything in aesthetic matters. It is just that such agreement does not often involve our agreeing that a certain proposition is true. And this can give the impression, even to the participants, that the disagreement was not resolved. Rather the impression we most often have, when we succeed, is that the disagreement was never around to be resolved. But in any case, the mere fact that some disagreements are never resolved does not mean that they never can be resolved. Or that there isn't a true answer which we shall perhaps one day find or understand.

Still, when we extract these confusions, there does appear to be a thought left which seems to get something unambiguously right. We can now examine this.

what aesthetic disagreement is (often) like

When we ascribe incompatible properties to works of art, we often do resolve the disagreement. Still, there are disagreements which are never resolved. And when we examine these disagreements we may see that they can never be resolved. For it may be that *nothing* that one person can say makes a difference to the other. The one just does not see the point of the other's remarks.

So, someone says 'Try hearing it like this' and he makes a certain gesture with his arm, perhaps waves it in a certain way.

And we hear some music playing and see a man waving his arm about. Or someone points to a part of the painting and looks back to us. She makes an expression with her mouth and eyes. Perhaps she frowns in a particular way. Then she says 'Look, can't you see..?' And we look and we can't.

And we know what it is like to be on the other side of this too. One can feel as if the other must be blind or deaf – 'Why does he not *want* to see this?!' As the theme is about to return, we look at them, smiling, encouraging them, telling them, 'Yes, you'll hear it now, here it comes..., here it is...now!', and then perhaps we swing our arms forward. Then...'Well, yes, I *suppose* I see what you mean,' and then quickly, 'Who did you say it was by?' And we are heartbroken. They didn't see that our gesture was *inside* the music. They didn't see that our gesture was a *reason* for hearing the notes in that way. And so perhaps we lower our eyes and play something we like less.

It is probably true to say that in most people's experience, this is most often what aesthetic disagreement is like: little trading of arguments, perhaps no assenting to and dissenting from propositions, little leading of people from agreed 'descriptions' of the work through to 'evaluations', hardly any syllogisms. Instead, we do not see the point of what someone else is seeing or hearing. And we are not able to get them to see and hear and move in, what is to us, the inside of the work. And when we reflect, we feel that through these experiences, frustrating as they often are, we learn something important about the character of aesthetic phenomena and especially of works of art.

aesthetic knowledge
Aesthetic disagreements are neither resolved nor resolvable in the way that disagreements elsewhere are neither resolved nor are they resolvable. This makes us feel that agreement in matters of aesthetics, and hence about works of art, is not as it is elsewhere. We feel that this affects the character of what it is to come to know something through aesthetic attention; the character of aesthetic knowledge.

We might think of it this way. Knowledge in physics or

knowledge about ordinary matters of fact (Is that Mercury? Whose turn is it to wash up?) may be acquired in different sorts of ways. But still it is all the same sort of knowledge. It all involves knowing that something is the case. It is not a different kind of knowledge because it is knowledge about the movement of the planets rather than about who has done their share of chores. What the evidence, beliefs, reasons and consequences are – all this is different in each case. But the sorts of relations there are between these things are the same.

Again, driving a car is very different from mountaineering, but when someone knows how to drive a car she has the *same sort of knowledge* that someone has when he knows how to abseil. It's just that it is concerned with very different activities. In the cases of knowing truths and in knowing how to do things, the character of the respective kinds of knowledge is not affected by what it is knowledge of or about.

But when we consider what agreement and disagreement are like in aesthetics we feel that the knowledge that an audience in the arts has is not only about different sorts of objects. It is a different sort of knowledge. Knowledge in aesthetics is unlike knowledge in physics and in horse-riding. For the sort of knowledge that an audience of art comes to have of works of art is tied to the nature of what it is they come to know: to the nature of works of art.

Aesthetic knowledge is special; it is *sui generis*, of its own kind. This is because it is conditioned by its objects. It is this that we feel has to be captured in any account of the relation between art and its audience.

This seems to be the thought left when we sort through all the questions with which we opened this chapter. Understood correctly, this thought is true. But it admits of two sorts of interpretation. And these interpretations lead in quite different directions and to quite different conceptions of the business of enjoying works of art.

aesthetic knowledge and self-knowledge

Some people will think it means this. They will say:
   'It is true that reflection on aesthetic agreement and

disagreement shows us that knowledge through our experience of works of art is not like knowledge elsewhere. It is a special kind of knowledge. It is the special sort of knowledge called knowledge of appearances.

'Where two people say incompatible things about a work of art – for example, about *Equivalent VIII* – what they jointly say cannot be true of this work. It cannot be both that in this work Andre has made a wonderful piece of sculpture and that what he has produced is bunk. But, if we assume that both people are sincere and since there is no way to *prove* that either person is wrong, then we must conclude that neither is talking about the object called *Equivalent VIII*. Rather, each is talking about how the object appears to them. And what each says is true of this appearance. They are not actually talking about the same thing but about two different things.

'But if this is true when we "disagree", it is also true when we "agree". So knowledge here is not like public knowledge. It is a kind of private knowledge. Where people do all agree about aesthetic matters what exists is only a kind of coincidence of knowledge over different appearances.

'So aesthetic interest is concerned with appearance and since appearances are not things in the world but things in the mind, I can only ever be interested in my appearances. I can't have what you see or hear or feel. And this explains everything there is to explain about our experience of works of art.

'It explains first of all why it can be so difficult to get others to agree with what we want to say about a work of art. And why we don't know why it sometimes happens that we like or dislike the same things. In these cases there is nothing to know – it is just a fact that we are similar in that sort of way. We can't know because in the sense in which the mind is private, all works of art are private. A work of art is essentially a special sort of occasion for private aesthetic experiences and reflections on those experiences.

'Second, and to return to the theme of the earlier chapter, this is why it does not really matter that we know what the artist intended. For what the artist thinks of his work is just what he thinks of another appearance of the work. This, by the way, is what is meant by saying that a great work of art is inexhaustible: a work of art is an indefinitely large set of possible appearances.

'This is also what is meant by the autonomy of a work of art. Its capacity to take on its own life, independent of its maker. For when an artist puts his work in the public realm, she is in effect saying, "Look, take this, see what you make of it. No. It's yours now; take this, make what you will of it." And this is what we do. We make partly what we can of it and partly what we will of it. And this depends in part on what it is and in part on what we are. Sorting out what aspects are which is not a philosophical matter. But only a matter of history or biography.'

Someone with this view might continue: 'So from the point of view of the people who really matter, the audience, works of art, certainly in the visual arts, are really no different in kind from aesthetically interesting natural objects. And what should be recognised is that to treat the artist's works in this way, is not to slight her. First, because when they have finished a piece, artists often talk this way themselves about their work. And second, because to do so is to acknowledge the artist's real achievement. Her power as an artist is to be able to make something which, while it has so many more sorts of qualities that we do not find or only very rarely find in nature, can yet be regarded as a natural object. The true artist lets us see through the art to something more important. She has made something wholly real. This quality, like that of a rock or an ocean, is what we mean by the inevitability we find in a great painting or piece of sculpture.

'It will be admitted that such an account is more difficult to make sense of in terms of other media of art. This is especially true of literature and poetry. But it is, after all, a consequence of this view that we ought not to expect an account which brings together the arts in terms of the same or closely related concepts to be either possible or, for that matter, desirable.

'And this is why it is pointless to seek a general description (other than saying this!) of what sort of thing a work of art is. Or, in general and without proceeding inductively through examples, to seek to describe what sort of difference there is between art and bunk. It is pointless because the first and last thing to say about aesthetic knowledge is that it is knowledge of appearances. And this means that aesthetic knowledge is, at its centre, a species of personal knowledge – of self-knowledge.'

This is how someone might go forward from the true thought that knowledge in aesthetics is not like knowledge elsewhere because of the nature of works of art.

aesthetic knowledge and knowledge of persons

There is, however, another way to understand this claim. We can think of it as being shorthand for three thoughts which are related but which may best be considered separately.

First, though knowing how to do certain things may be a condition of acquiring it, aesthetic knowledge is not knowing how to do something. It does centrally involve coming to know truths. But, at the same time, aesthetic knowledge on the part of an audience does not consist in their assenting to or dissenting from true statements; from particular propositions.

So, a fellow might know that such and such a sculptor is highly thought of by those whose job it is to think highly of such sculptors. That the sculptor ought to be highly thought of may be true. And the explanations of why this is may be true.

But if our fellow has not seen the sculpture, or worse, if he does not let himself see the sculpture because he has been told these truths, then he has so far done nothing that has anything to do with aesthetics. Merely to repeat the propositions that truly specify the value of the work whilst standing in front of the work is not to get anywhere. He has, as it were, merely mouthed seeing the sculpture.

If he does not speak for himself about this work, then he does not speak at all.

But this is not to say that he cannot have used their words and their explanations to guide what he sees, to enable him to see something he would not otherwise have seen. Nor that he cannot agree with the words of others or use the words of others to describe what he sees. To speak for himself is not to speak against others. It is only that he must come to see that the point of what is said is, as it were, inside the seeing of the work. The true words must stand to the seeing of the work not, say, as the diagnosis stands to being ill but as holding the part that hurts stands to being injured.

This is only to point out that the meaning of the words that specify the value of the sculptor's work is connected with the point of uttering them. Someone who has no conception of the point of uttering the words cannot be said to understand the truth of what is said.

However, this does not mean that what is at stake is the kind of knowledge that consists in having something. For example, the kind of knowledge that we think we have when we are in pain.

For, if we think this, we will cast round for something connected with the work but which, like the pain, is something we can *have*. And we latch upon the appearance of the object to us as something over and above how the object appears. This knowledge of appearance, in being certain, seems the best sort of knowledge and yet in being private, seems not like knowledge at all; certainly not like communicable knowledge. And so now art and aesthetic knowledge will seem very mysterious.

But there is nothing mysterious in denying that aesthetic knowledge consists in knowing that certain statements – propositions – are true. First of all, it is far from clear that there is any knowledge that can be described simply as knowing that individual propositions are true. Even in the hard sciences, which are in these respects alternately lauded and damned by comparison with the arts, knowledge does not consist in knowing that this proposition is true, and this one, and this one too. Knowledge comes in networks, and not every part of the network needs to be articulated.

But secondly, we need not say there is anything mysterious here because we are all perfectly familiar with another sphere in which there is just this sort of knowledge, and yet where we feel there is no mystery. Or where, if there is a mystery, then we have no difficulty in seeing that it is a quite general one and so not one peculiar to aesthetics. This sphere is our knowledge of persons, our knowledge of each other.

In this sphere, what greater difference could there be than that between knowing some true propositions about someone and knowing them? But we don't think that therefore we *don't* know any truths about anybody.

Nor do we think that because knowledge of true propositions is not at the centre of knowledge of persons, that therefore it is the kind of knowing that consists in having something, perhaps the impression that the person makes upon us. That therefore a friend is nothing over and above the sum of the impressions he makes upon others. Few are so crass as to believe that this is what we mean when we talk about the inexhaustible human soul; that someone may strike us all differently.

We don't think this because we see that the sort of knowledge we have here is the sort of knowledge we have through being things. We have knowledge in being someone in relation to others. We have knowledge through being their friends and relatives and enemies and lovers.

Again, when it comes to making judgements about others, say their moral character, in what sense are we able to prove anything? Sometimes we can 'prove' things. In a court of law we might say that all the evidence points to his having been of irreproachable integrity. But even here this is not like proof in science or proof in mathematics. Other times we can't prove things. But then often we are not at all concerned to prove what we say in that sort of way. We are only trying to get you to see that he wasn't meaning to be rude. It's not in him to be rude like that. If you can't see this, maybe we just have to accept it. But none of this means that we think that there is no being correct or incorrect here.

We might say that knowledge in the sphere of human relations is not like knowledge elsewhere. That such knowledge is *sui generis* because it is knowledge of persons. It is a sort of knowledge that is conditioned by what human beings are. But this does not make us feel that there is anything intrinsically impossible in understanding some important things about human relationships, about, for example, what sort of difference there is between friendship and betrayal.

Consideration of this sphere, then, shows us that we should not be misled by analogous features in our experience of works of art. In particular, this aspect of the claim that knowledge in aesthetics is not like knowledge elsewhere – that aesthetic knowledge on the part of an audience does not consist in assenting to or dissenting from propositions – can now be seen to be true without committing us to a quite unwarranted view: that aesthetic knowledge simply *is* knowledge of persons – self-knowledge.

aesthetic knowledge and aesthetic competence

The idea that aesthetic knowledge is not like knowledge elsewhere is shorthand for a second claim: the proper object of aesthetic attention in a work of art is not something like its frame or its canvas, something of a once and for all specifiable size and depth and extent. This is why knowledge of it is not like knowledge of the size of bits of wood, or the weight of a lump of canvas.

But this does not mean that therefore we are dealing with something private or peculiar to the minds of those who see or hear the work. The popular dictum cheats here – we think the eye a harmless proxy for the mind of the beholder. But by using this metaphor the saying appeals to illusions about vision to support confusions about art. If we say the ear of the listener, or better still the hand of the toucher (think of ceramics or certain sorts of sculpture) we are suddenly brought up short. Beauty is in the hand of the toucher. How could this be true? When we consider touch, we are not nearly so prone to strip what is felt from the object – to privatise what properly belongs in public ownership.

What this claim does mean is something perfectly ordinary and yet also illuminating for the business of enjoying works of art.

What counts as the appearance of a work of art is something relative to a background of competence, a background with many different levels often intermingling in complicated ways.

an innocent at the Tate

To illustrate this point, think of the following as something like a fable or a joke.

Imagine that some time after all the furore over *Equivalent VIII*, an innocent decides to go to the Tate Gallery in London in order to find out something about *Equivalent VIII* for himself. What does he need to know? What does he need to be able to do?

A man goes to the Tate. Freeze.

This is different from playing a record or watching a play on video or reading a copy of *Under Milk Wood*. Whatever it is, its importance does not seem to consist in something that can be copied or digitised or transmitted. Understanding *Equivalent VIII* involves being in the same place as it. Why this is so is of course not yet apparent. Perhaps it is for the same sort of reason one prefers to go to a concert or the theatre. It's so much better than a recording or a broadcast that it verges on the altogether different. But beneath this is another important background idea. For what so much as gives our friend the idea that this *Equivalent VIII* ought or ought not to be compared with music or drama or poetry? Why are these relevant comparisons? Well, perhaps our innocent knows nothing of these other media and is not surprised at having to go somewhere especially to see *Equivalent VIII*.

So, he arrives at the Tate. Freeze.

Here is the idea of an institution which is charged with looking after *Equivalent VIII*. This is curious. One does not look after plays and novels and pieces of music in this way. More or less, they look after themselves. And is this institution publicly funded? Public funding is usually devoted only to what is deemed necessary for the public good. Is *Equivalent VIII* necessary for the public good? Is this thing deemed to be valuable? Or only things of this type? Perhaps he will discover when he goes in and finds *Equivalent VIII*.

He enters the gallery, checks in his coat and asks the way. The first thing he notices are the people. They are talking very softly. Freeze.

What kind of hush is this? Is this hush for the sake of

privacy and concentration, like in a library? Or is it for respect and reverence, as in a church?

If we let the story continue, we can get some idea of the range of things that our innocent needs to know and of what he needs to be able to do.

When he eventually gets there, he almost falls over it. What a place to leave it lying around! Why isn't it on the wall with the rest? Still, here it is. Now what was all the fuss about? He looks around a little more and sees a small white card. He notices that people keep coming along and looking at the thing on the floor and then looking around and then looking down some more. And though nothing much happens, one thing that strikes him is that people keep snatching glances at the small white card and then quickly look away. They look positively guilty as if they shouldn't be looking at the card. Maybe it's rude. Or maybe it's a secret which somehow spoils the thing for people. But no, if it were, it wouldn't be on the wall. So for the sake of something to do, he reads it. It says *Equivalent VIII* – he's got the right one then – and then has someone's name followed by some measurements and something about some bricks. Well, he can see it's made of bricks. But who found it? Perhaps the man named on the card. He wonders if this man found any other flat rectangular things. Our innocent spends some time thinking about flat hard objects. He thinks of long lines of timber blocks. Of steel plates. He thinks about different ways of arranging these blocks and plates. But he quickly gets bored with this and he decides instead to count the number of bricks on the floor. 120. Not a *very* interesting number. And then for a time he thinks about bricks. He wonders how they are made. How much they cost to make. How much a brickmaker gets paid. Not enough probably. Not as much as the person who sells the bricks, anyway.

And then nothing much happens for quite a long time. The chap mentioned on the card obviously wasn't coming today which was a shame because he would like to have asked him where he found the object and what it was for. And so he looks at the bricks a bit more. He falls to wondering if there is anything marked on the bottom of the bricks, the side on the floor. But just as he bends down to investigate a soldier walks right past him and gives him one hell of a dirty look.

And so he thinks better of it and after checking the card again, just in case he missed anything, he falls to looking at the bricks once more. And it seems to him a funny thing but the more he looks at it, the more he starts thinking about how flat it is. It really is very low and flat. Not very high at all when you compared it with how high the things on the wall are. And then a moment of panic. Oh God – perhaps it's fallen *off* the wall. He hopes the soldier doesn't blame him. But then the bricks would have to be stuck together and he is not absolutely sure, just from the look of them, that they are stuck together. He'd like to check but that soldier is coming back again.

So he continues to think about flat things, roads and the bottoms of irons and water. And now he falls to thinking about water some more, and especially of a lake he sailed on this time last summer. It was just like a mirror. The land is never flat like a mirror. He very much enjoyed thinking about that lake and how nice it was sailing on it and how very, very flat it was. But apart from the lake, and irons of course, things being flat didn't seem all that important really. On the whole he was getting a bit fed up, waiting for *Equivalent VIII* to start.

Overall, and apart from thinking about the lake and how flat it was, the event or the thing or whatever it was wasn't doing very much for him. On the whole, he'd rather have gone rowing on the lake again. But perhaps he's got it wrong. Perhaps he was supposed to do things to it.

Then suddenly it occurs to him what he is supposed to do. What a fool! He has, after all, had some extremely interesting thoughts about flat things and lakes and the difference between the water and the land. And about bricks and how they are made. And who makes them. And who makes money from them. And why those two groups of people aren't the same. And he sees now that this *Equivalent VIII* is beautifully rectangular and flat. Just like a sheet of paper. He will write on its lovely flat surface everything it has made him think about. That was probably why the soldier was getting mad. 'Get on with it' he was saying. 'Get it all down quickly and give someone else a chance.' And so he takes his best fountain pen from his pocket. He wants to make a neat job of this. It will match the neatness of the bricks, laid out in lines. Like trains. But trains only look like that seen from above. That's another interesting thought. That should go on too. But just then the pen slips from his hand, falls, breaks on the bricks, and he watches helpless as the ink spreads slowly around and then down, down through the cracks in *Equivalent VIII*.

A silly story, of course. But what differences would there really be if our innocent went to find not Andre's work but Constable's, or Michelangelo's?

levels of competence

The different levels of competence are summarised in the diagram (see Figure 2). At the most fundamental level are those capacities which depend upon deep facts about the sorts of creature we are. We could not have works of art, they could not be a type of thing which people produced or which people enjoyed, if our responses to such things as colours, or size, clutteredness, resolution of tension, volume and so on, were always and only matters for individual decision. Our responses to such qualities are not reducible to neurophysiology but nothing is more obvious than that they presuppose it.

Further up, so to speak, is our relation to a whole set of values, archetypes, ways of going on in thought and action, whose influence is everywhere and, because of this, whose character is problematic. For we do not know if they belong to human culture or only to our culture. Think, for example, of what it is to be responsive to the sort of difference we find between minor and major keys. Is the possibility of responding to such a difference something internal or external to the music of a culture? Are such responses specific to a music culture? Or is there enough structure in sound to treat this response as the expression of a far more general capacity? Again, what is it to hear a note as higher or lower than another? Is this something relatively culture-specific – like being able to make three-dimensional sense of flat patterns of line and tone? Or is it a metaphor built into the structure of human perception?

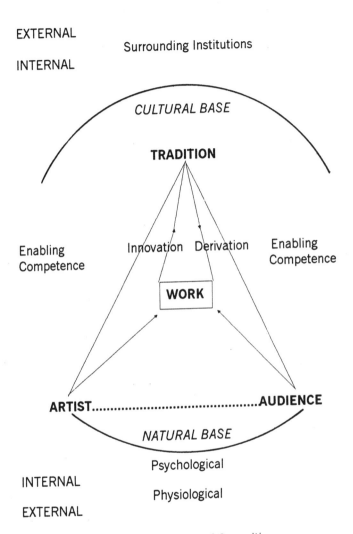

EXTERNAL

INTERNAL

Surrounding Institutions

CULTURAL BASE

TRADITION

Enabling
Competence

Innovation   Derivation

Enabling
Competence

WORK

ARTIST..**AUDIENCE**

NATURAL BASE

Psychological

INTERNAL

Physiological

EXTERNAL

Transcultural Shared Capacities

Figure 2

Think of number – of the different orders in 2 and in 3. Perhaps it is not clear to us in such cases just what this distinction between 'universal' and 'culture-specific' comes to.

And, of course, even where they are clearly culture-specific, such determinants penetrate downward. We feel that certain colours are transparent in their significance; the purity of a kind of white or the solemnity of tones of black. We feel it impossible to know green as the colour of grief. Yet in some cultures white has this role. In what way can this make sense to us?

Such elements also reach upwards into the specifics of a particular culture, its political and religious and iconographic inheritance, the media in which people have worked. They are then ploughed back into the particular histories of particular artists with concerns and preoccupations that are internal to art.

Because the capacities which enter into it have an enormous range in their degree of specificity, a concept of art is therefore in part physiologically, in part historically, and in part culturally determined. And these levels also mingle and interpenetrate in the most complex ways. Out of all this complexity there emerges a concept of what it is to look at a particular painting at a particular moment in history. Out of this massive complex of capacities, competences and familiarities, with their enormous range in degree of generality, it comes to be that now, in front of this painting, I am not at all inclined to look at the back of this thing suspended on the wall. Or perhaps it strikes me that this painting does not look as if it were made to be seen straight on. And I try looking at it from the side. And it makes a new kind of sense. That this is or isn't the right thing to do of course depends upon how the painting looks. But that it could or couldn't be something it makes sense to do depends upon the possibility of a rule or set of rules which tacitly guides what I can count as looking at this painting.

art rules
It is therefore a condition of recognising something as a work of art that it is possible for the production of the object to have been regulated by rules; rules which render the object possible

as a work. To be able to recognise a particular object as a work of art, so that this complex background becomes relevant, depends upon the fact that, in general, objects of this kind are producible according to rules. Only then will it be possible to say not that I don't feel like looking at the back of this painting but that it doesn't make sense to look at the back of this painting.

This is to say that the concept of a work of art as something distinct from either natural aesthetic objects or objects which just happen to have been made by someone, plays an active role in determining both the creation and the appreciation of art.

This is the notion of a regulative concept of art. Adopting this account of the concept of a work of art means leaving behind the philosophical enterprise of trying to describe the content of a concept of art for all times and places; the idea that the real function of art is religious or political or personal; that, necessarily, art must cherish or liberate or enrich. Instead, we must accord full importance to the fact that our concept of art is ours – a largely historically and culturally conditioned concept. Discovering what sorts of objects with what sorts of function a concept of art in a particular culture describes is a job for criticism or art history.

But adopting such an account also means recognising that there must be one element which is not historically conditioned: the content of the concept being employed must be capable of directing our aesthetic interest to the intended appearance of the work. For otherwise we would not need to distinguish between works of art and other objects of aesthetic interest.

Though this is a purely formal requirement, it has substantial implications for art history and criticism. If the concept of art, under which an object is produced, frustrates the best efforts of the audience to see the object as a work, as meant, then the object thereby fails to be a work of art. It is irrelevant that the object may, nevertheless, be beautiful, charming or intriguing. Natural objects may also be beautiful, charming or intriguing. It is equally irrelevant, as we have seen, that the object was, as a matter of fact, made by someone. This is true even if everyone is acquainted with this fact. What is relevant is that the knowledge that the object was made can serve as the starting point for finding it aesthetically intelligible: the object is capable of rewarding aesthetic interest in its intended appearance.

So while the content of this concept varies from medium to medium and may be highly culturally and historically variant, the formal role played by a concept of art is invariant and this places at least some restrictions on possible content. Indeed, in the context of the visual arts, this raises serious doubts about a number of traditions which seek actively to undermine the coherence of any distinction between works of art and natural or simply man-made aesthetic objects. We will return to this topic in the next chapter.

too intellectual?

For now it is worth considering one objection to what has been said so far. It may be objected that we are placing too great an emphasis on the idea of a regulative concept of art, resulting in an excessively intellectualist picture of our experience of works of art. In so doing we stress the role played by knowledge, belief and cognition at the expense of perception and experience. But since the aesthetic is essentially concerned with appearance, perception and experience are really central to aesthetic experience and any account that relegates them to a secondary role must be mistaken. What we know and what we believe must not be allowed to interfere with what we see and what we feel.

This last claim is correct. But it cannot be used to undermine the importance of the distinction between works of art and other sorts of objects of aesthetic attention. For the relegation of perception and experience to a secondary role is precisely what is wrong, not with our account, but with its opposite; with the sort of account which seeks to assimilate the sense of appearance relevant to our aesthetic interest in natural objects to the sense of appearance relevant to our interest in works of art. Whilst it may appear that perceptual experience is being given the primary role in such an account, this is only an illusion created by the fact that, on this model, perceptual capacities are exercised first but not foremost.

A useful way of thinking of this is summarised by the cartoon.

Model A   Model B

Some Hmms and Ahs about art.

ah...hmm!

On this account, Model A, there are three distinguishable stages in any encounter with a work of art. The first stage is indeed perceptual, with no trace of interference by cognitive processes. The object we encounter is an enigma to us. It could be any kind of object of aesthetic interest from a work of art in a particular medium, for example a painting, to an object which is of interest only if we approach it in the right frame of mind. We cannot say what sort of thing it is at all until we have explored it.

In the second stage of our encounter with the object, we notice the various aspects and features of the object. It is at this stage that there is supposed to occur whatever we understand by the notion of aesthetic experience. It is because of some feature or aspect of the object that we are delighted or enlightened or shocked or surprised. And this is a direct consequence of noticing particular features of the object. And now what?

In the third stage of this model we use the occurrence of this experience as a basis for inferring two conclusions. First, that the enigmatic object is in fact a work of art rather than some other sort of object and second, that it is this particular work of art: that, as a work of art, it has these particular values, these specific meanings, this sort of worth or lack of it.

But it is this third stage that shows that the account does not give precedence to the perceptual over the cognitive and intellectual. For on this account, the perceptual exploration, though it is the first stage, is not the most important. It is in fact merely preparatory to the main event. The main event is the inference from the experience to the realisation of just what this object is. One's relation to the object as this particular work of art consists in what one *thinks* or comes to *believe* when one has successfully drawn a conclusion from the nature of the experience one has just had. And this can be carried out with one's face turned away from the object. On this model, the perceptual is prior only in the sense that it is earlier. The cognitive is given logical priority.

Curiously then, on this model, the business of enjoying and understanding works of art is akin to the business of science. In science, experience, experiment, is important only as a means to an end: the development of theories. Similarly here. The assimilation of works of art to other sorts of objects and the failure to appreciate the role played by a background of competence lead to the conclusion that the understanding of a work of art must be conceived as a kind of theory about one's experience of the object.

What could be more inappropriately intellectualist than this?

hmm...ah!

On the sort of account that we have been concerned to put forward here, exactly the reverse is true. Knowledge and belief about a wide range of things are indeed prior. But only in the sense that such cognitive luggage is what we must have prepared beforehand if we want to go on this particular journey. And this means that at no stage are we under the impression that what we have before us might, for all we know, be a natural object and that we shall have to reserve judgement about this matter until we have carried out a proper inspection. So the account put forward here, Model B in the cartoon, distinguishes two stages in encounters with works of art.

First, we do not find some enigmatic we-know-not-what. This is because we do not often or really *find* such things. For the most part works of art find us. Perhaps we hear about them and then we seek them out. We know what sort of thing the object is before we look *at* it because very often we have been looking *for* it. And so, what we seek out is a painting or a piece of sculpture or a play or a novel. And we now know or can find out who made this thing, roughly when, roughly under what sorts of relevant conditions. And so on. As we have seen, just what sort of thing we must know in advance here is not itself determined in advance.

But whatever is involved at this stage is essentially cognitive. It involves having beliefs, recalling other works, almost certainly it involves reflection on one's culture and the history of that culture. It may mean exercising very simple, or perhaps extremely complex, skills. If we do not know who made this thing, we may need skills as simple as that of reading the signature of the artist on the canvas. Or we may need skills as complicated as those involved in having the canvas carbon-dated. All this is essentially cognitive. But the point of all this is not essentially cognitive.

What this makes possible is the second stage of the encounter. It makes it possible for us to be in the right sort of position in relation to this object. And having succeeded in achieving an appropriate orientation in regard to the object, we may now be in position to see this particular painting in all its specificity. And this, the point of all that happens, is an essentially perceptual business.

So the point of having the relevant beliefs and bits of knowledge, of knowing something about the history of this activity, of theories about art, of all the various capacities and cultural predispositions, the relevance of all this background across its whole range, is not to enable us to construct theories about special sorts of objects. It is to enable us to see. Or to hear. Or to feel.

The objection, then, is misconceived. To stress the relevance of this background with all the many beliefs and sorts of abilities it involves is not to present an excessively intellectualist picture of our understanding of works of art. On the contrary, it is to insist that the articulation of such beliefs and the acquisition of such abilities are not allowed to become the point of the whole activity: that, in all their multiplicity, they remain as back-ground.

And this is what can be so difficult, so frustrating in talking with others about works of art. For we must feel able to rely on this background, able to call out expressions of recognition from others. I may, therefore, be unable to describe an aesthetic difference to you because I do not know what aspect of this background of competence and capacity I am appealing to. And if I do know, to have to describe it to you may already be to lose the point of doing so. My confidence in the sense of the descriptions and interpretations I offer may depend upon my feeling secure that the relevant aspects of this background can go unspoken and unquestioned.

So the idea that what counts as the intended appearance of a work of art is something relative to a background of competence is not an excessively intellectualist conception of our experience of art. It is part of what we mean by saying that works of art determine the sort of knowledge it is possible to have of them.

aesthetic knowledge and aesthetic agreement

There is a third idea which is part of the claim that knowledge in matters of aesthetics is conditioned by the nature of works of art; what counts as agreement in aesthetics is also something conditioned by its objects. This idea leads to what is perhaps the most important thing to understand about the relation between works of art and their audience.

Someone who had accepted what we have said so far might now think this. 'In the end, doesn't all this lead the same way? Does any of this make a ha'p'orth of difference to the essential truth? That, in the end, the difference between art and bunk is what people think it is. And people can disagree.

'We should accept that of course there will be disagreements. People have both different non-aesthetic interests and different aesthetic interests. But this does not mean that we say what we like. It doesn't mean that the object is just an engine for generating appearances or that such an object may as well be a natural object. For there is, in practice, a very great deal of agreement about works of art. Most works of art can only be produced against such a background of agreement. And disagreement, when it is interesting, is interesting because of this background.

'Let it be allowed that in order to be able to see something as a work of art, we must allow a whole range of background capacities and competence to guide and inform our present perception. At all its different levels of specificity, this represents a concept of art for that culture and this allows us to see the intended appearance of the work.

'Let us be happy with the idea that a concept of art has different levels of specificity, that its broad base is founded in quite general capacities and that its apex may point to this work with all its particularities of time and place and intention. The only limits here are the limits we find in practice and the criterion of relevance is only what can make a difference to what is seen. This is true of the artist too. Such a concept guides and regulates what is seen for artist and audience.

'But now, if the capacity to be able to see this pile of bricks as a piece of sculpture depends upon my being able to see it here and now with this concept in place, then was it not right all along to insist that what counts as this work of art is something which depends upon me? For isn't it the case that people will, as it were, stand at different levels within this concept? Someone who brings more or less will see more or less.

'But still we will both have every right to claim that what we each see is really the work. On this view, more so than before! For we have now abandoned the idea that the real work of art is just the sum of its appearances. Each of us can say that what we see, relative to a concept of art that we bring with us, really is the work of art. And doesn't this mean that what sort of thing a work of art is depends upon us?

'And isn't this the central and the only really important truth in aesthetics? For while there is in fact a great deal of agreement, absolutely nothing guarantees this. There is nothing in all this that guarantees that the audiences of art will go on seeing the same sort of thing in the same sort of way.

laughing at Lear

'What is there in the following that speaks against this possibility. You are watching the last scene of a titanic production. Lear enters, Cordelia in his arms. In the aisle in front of you, a portly gentleman begins to fidget uncomfortably, distracting your eye. As Lear reaches centre stage, the portly spectator twists from side to side, his shoulders begin to heave up and down. And then unable to contain himself any more, he explodes into great belly aches of laughter, gesturing helplessly towards the stage. When we question him everything he says points to his having seen and heard what we saw and heard. He was attentive, interested and so on. And yet he finds it funny.

'We could of course try to find out what kind of funny this was. But there is no certainty that his answer will change anything. Perhaps he says, 'Oh, you know – funny like a practical joke – like slipping on a banana – *classically funny*'.

'We may say, if we can, that his laughing proves that he does not understand *King Lear*. And, indeed, if there were always a *logical* connection between understanding a work of art and reacting in a certain way then this would be the sort of cast-iron guarantee that we need. We could show him what kind of mistake he had made. But it is very hard to say that this *is* a kind of mistake. It is surely not that he has made a false inference, or has simply got the wrong end of the stick. If someone were to react in this way, where would we start with him? What if he always reacted in this sort of way? What could we point to? We would be all at sea.

'But if this is a possibility for an audience then there is nothing that guarantees that they will remain an audience. For however beautiful they are, a sunrise or an ocean or a shaft of light catching the handle of a knife do not have audiences, only groups of people enjoying how they appear to them, perhaps in very different ways. And, if there are no absolute limits on what counts as understanding a work of art, then, there is nothing here that guarantees that works of art cannot in fact come to be treated by everyone as if they were natural objects. And this would be an end to the notion of art. This possibility is really what we mean by saying that the sort of thing a work of art is depends upon us.'

This is how someone might think. And it is correct. It wants, we might say, only a change in the tone of voice with which it is said for this to be a solution to our problem about the relation between works of art and their audience. Again the analogy with human relations may transform things.

What reorientates our thinking about this is seeing that the thought that our portly fellow *cannot* understand *King Lear* is of a piece with the thought that we *do not* understand *him*. For, outside of aesthetics, we are familiar with the thought that someone may be as close to the completely unintelligible as something which looks like a human being can be. But this does not undermine our own position. The moral monster is both disturbing and problematic but he ought not to make us look queerly at our children.

In our knowledge of each other, we accept that there is no home for the thought that we live in the lack of binding guarantees. We are secure as needs be in the thought that we will go on, mostly, understanding each other and making sense to each other. No one actually feels, in their relations with others, that everything must be built on super-rigid foundations. The possibility of human communication is not, as a matter of fact, guaranteed by logic. Nor, so to speak, is it logically guaranteed by the facts. Its possibility does not depend upon such things. It is this general thought about human communication that we need to reorientate our thinking about the relation between art and audience.

It means that the only real and honest answer to the question of whether there might cease to be an audience for art because there might cease to be agreement about art is: Yes, this might happen. But the limits of what it is that we can count as understanding a work of art are marked by the same flags and fences as those which delimit the people we can make sense of. The limits of aesthetic understanding are therefore akin to the limits of our understanding of each other.

This also means that, just as it is possible, by accident or design, to undermine and confound our relations with each other, so it is possible to fragment and destroy a concept of art. The resistance to this process embedded in the traditions of art, and the implications of the existence of such traditions for the sorts of contrast that need to be drawn between art and bunk, form the theme of our next chapter.

notes

p.62. A useful anthology of artists' views about art is *Theories of Modern Art: A Source Book by Artists and Critics*, Herschel Chipp (Berkeley, University of California Press, 1968). The view that aesthetics has no real philosophical job to do found its classic expression in *Language, Truth and Logic*, A.J. Ayer (Harmondsworth, Penguin, 1971) p. 150.

p.63. The view that aesthetic theories are primarily ways of preparing for changes in taste can be found in 'Does Traditional Aesthetics Rest on a Mistake?', W.E. Kennick in *Mind* 1958 pp. 317-34.

p.87. The diagram is adapted with permission from one originally designed by Kjell S. Johannessen for his article 'Art and Aesthetic Praxis' in *Contemporary Aesthetics in Scandinavia*, edited by Lars Aagaard-Mongensen and Goran Hermeren (Lund, Sweden, Bokforlaget Doxa AB, 1980).

p.98. There is a useful discussion of aberrant reactions to works of art in 'Text and Context', Peter Winch in *Philosophical Investigations*, January, 1981 pp. 42-56.

4: art and tradition

Is the sort of difference there is between art and bunk determined by an object's relations to the traditions of art? Or rather, since we have already come across some differences, determined by things other than tradition, are there *sorts* of difference between art and bunk that are determined by tradition; by the relation of an object to the history of works of art? If something is to be a work of art, must it stand in some particular sort of relation to this history? And, conversely, if something fails to be a work of art can this be because it is in some way defective or lacking or compromised in its relations to this history?

Just to begin, let us tell ourselves a philosophical fable. We will not dwell on the story. But we can think of the rest of the chapter as its moral.

tra

Imagine that you are an interstellar explorer who has stumbled across a hitherto undiscovered civilisation in a distant solar system. The inhabitants are humanoid in appearance and appear to live in ways which, in many respects at least, seem familiar from life on Earth. Since (in the best science fiction tradition) they speak a language which is miraculously close to English, you are able to communicate with them. You find that though they have no interest in leaving their home planet, they are quite used to visitors from other worlds and treat you with that mixture of courtesy and indifference reserved everywhere in the galaxy especially for dealing with tourists.

Imagine now that exploring one of their large cities, you find near its centre a curious building that seems to have no obvious residential, technological or administrative function. Inside is a large hall half-filled with people. Apart from a few hushed whispers there is little or no conversation. In the middle of the hall and at the centre of everyone's attention, there is what seems to you to be a very curious object, resting on a large platform or plinth. It is a large plain cube made of a translucent, alabaster-like substance. Each side of the cube is marked with a series of engraved lines at equal spaces. There are no other features you can discern. People spend most of their time looking at this object from every angle. They walk around it, occasionally nodding in a way it seems natural to call 'appreciatively'. Finally they leave the room, mostly in meditative silence, but occasionally you hear them whisper to their friends 'How beautiful, how very beautiful'. As they leave, others enter and behave in the same sort of way.

You discover that the function of other rooms in the building is only to service the main hall and its visitors. There are cafes, cloakrooms and so on. In one room you discover people buying pictures of the object: from small postcards to large elegantly framed photographs. There are also small replicas of the object on sale.

Later, consulting your appointed guide, you discover that the object is of the home culture and known to be very old. It seems that every large city has an identical ancient object in a special building near its centre. When you press your guide on the origins of these objects, however, he becomes first puzzled and then reticent. Somehow he just doesn't seem interested in your questions. When you insist that he answers, his reticence turns suddenly to anger and he exclaims 'Look, who cares about where they came from? Can't you see – their history is irrelevant. They are for *being with*, nothing else. Don't you have Tra where you come from?'

Finally realising the significance of the objects, you start to ask more specific questions – what qualities do they admire it for? – what is its particular significance or meaning? – who are the leading authorities on it? – where can you see other works of 'Tra'? You are interrupted by howling laughter. 'You're so funny, you aliens. If we were able to talk about the significance of Tra there would be no point in having it. Just *be* with it – it is what it is. As for "other works of Tra" I can't understand what you mean. How *can* there be other Tra's?'

To think about whether or not the alien object could be a work of art is to think about whether two other sorts of object are works of art.

The cave paintings of Lascaux would only have been reached after a dangerous descent. As far as is known, they would only have been seen by the light of torches. The best guess about their purpose seems to be that they played some role in an important mystical or religious ritual. Everything around them speaks against their having anything in common with what we think we understand as works of art. Yet, for all that, what could look more like works of art?

Equivalent VIII could be reached quite easily after moving through the Tate entrance. It was well lit and surrounded by many objects widely agreed to be works of art. Critical and historical descriptions and interpretations were freely available. Everything around it spoke in favour of its having everything in common with what we think we understand as a work of art. Yet, for all that, what could look less like a work of art?

Is what can count as a work of art determined by history?

The first thing to say here is that this is a question on which there are well established and mutually antagonistic points of view. The conflict between these points of view has greatly influenced the creation of works in the visual arts as parts of those amalgams of doctrine, practice and accident which are known as Modernism and Late Modernism. Since it is just such works, particularly those of Late Modernism, which have tended most to invite accusations about a failure to distinguish art from bunk, it is worth saying something about this debate right away.

a larger battle

To many philosophers, critics and artists, the question of the relation between the nature of a work of art and the traditions of art has seemed to be an important skirmish in a battle over much larger issues.

On one side, to several related schools of thought it has seemed important to show that what we understand by something's being a work of art is indeed determined by the traditions of art. But this is so because such traditions are themselves historically determined, which is to say they are determined by just the sorts of process that determine history. Showing this is important not only for what it tells us about works of art but also because it tells us something about history and historical processes and what else must be determined in this way, if works of art are.

The thought here is that if even what counts as a work of art is determined by history, what of any real importance will not be?

Equally, those who are opposed to this view have thought that to show that there is something essential to the notion of a work of art which is *not* determined by what has happened to us and our cultures, also gives us an insight into something over and above the nature of works of art. It shows some such thing as that we do not live in the causal inheritance of the past alone. If the values and interests inherent in works of art are not essentially conditioned by history, then it is at least possible that there exist other sorts of values and interests which are not conditioned by history.

The equal and opposite thought here is that if what counts as a work of art is not essentially dependent on history, what of any real importance need be?

In this way, whether or not we can regard works of art as in some sense essentially conditioned by history comes to be perceived as a test case for larger issues. This is why it is supposed to matter what we say about the cave paintings and *Equivalent VIII*.

Each side accuses the other of similar sins. And we can gain an understanding of the issues by exploring these charges and the arguments brought forward to support them. It will be best here to adopt the voice of each point of view.

history isn't essential

Those who think that history is essential are charged with oppressive and restrictive politicisation, hubris, and worst of all, inattention to the phenomena of art and in particular to the autonomy of works of art.

First, those committed to the essentially historical character of works of art are principally motivated, not by the desire to understand the character of aesthetic interest, but by the wish to politicize activities – the production and understanding of works of art – which are too important and certainly too various to fit inside any particular political ideology.

Second, those committed to this view are bewitched by the supposed power of their system of explanation. Such is the pride in the system that whatever does not fit must be reduced to something that will fit. And this is simply not appropriate to the phenomena of art. For the overwhelming impression that aesthetic phenomena make upon us is first their sheer range and diversity, and, second, their difference from any other kind of phenomena.

When we reflect on why this reductionism is completely alien to aesthetics, we can see that this is a consequence of the fact that works of art are not essentially historical. For given their variety, the only way it seems even plausible to theorize about aesthetic phenomena is to investigate not what examples of aesthetic phenomena have in common but rather what we have in common when we are attending in the proper way to such phenomena. And thinking about what our experience is like here must mean putting historical matters in parenthesis. For the sort of interest we have in works of art is rooted in the sort of aesthetic interest we take in natural objects. And this latter is too obviously transcultural a capacity to be in any really interesting way historically conditioned.

This shows us the true importance of the history of art for understanding the character of its objects. The relevant connection between works of art and tradition is not that, through tradition, history determines what counts as a work of art. It is rather, first, that of course, history in part determines what sort of works of art we have in a particular time. But, second, and more important, the study of history tells us what works of art are always like. History does not make works of art what they are. It is evidence for what works of art really are.

Thus the study of past art shows us just how often what appear to be culture-specific values and practices are founded in quite general, transhistorical capacities and interests. So if our own painters concern themselves with representation and expression in their work, this is because these are the general human capacities relevant to painting. Painting is rooted in seeing and feeling and imagining. This is how, despite the particular values they may have had in that culture, it makes sense to think of cave paintings as works of art.

Finally, it is just because of the threat that the autonomy of these activities poses to such supposedly complete systems of explanation that attempts to include artistic activities within them proceed with such complete disregard for the phenomena themselves. For, even if it is conceded that such accounts did have true explanations of the origins of aesthetic phenomena in the material conditions of human life, still this would not explain the nature of such activities – their point, their value. There are two reasons for this. Both are connected with the idea of aesthetic autonomy; the logical independence of aesthetic phenomena from any other kind of phenomena.

First, we ought not to accept as relevant causal explanations of what is an essentially *normative* phenomenon (i.e one involving values). However we describe the value of aesthetic phenomena such as works of art – whether we think entirely in formal terms or bring to bear moral or even spiritual concepts – we are acquainted with these values only through the experience of them. Like being a moral agent, the point of the activity is simply not intelligible to someone who is on the outside, looking in. It is clear only to those on the inside, looking in. If you want to know why the fine perspective afforded on the park is a reason for sitting here then everything you do is logically irrelevant until you come and sit down and look. Our apprehension of the value of aesthetic phenomena is logically independent of other activities. So explanations of this value in terms of anything else are not relevant.

Secondly (this line of critique continues), even if causal explanations could be relevant, it is far from clear that works of art have value in the sort of way that would be required. For example, it might be argued that different acts of courage are all valuable for the same sort of reason. If so, we may offer an explanation of the sort of value that courageous acts have. But it may be that it is a mistake to regard aesthetic experience as having some value over and above the particular aesthetic values discovered in the course of the experience of particular objects. Why must the values of a Cezanne be related to the values we find in the sculpture of David Smith? Why should we think that there must be some *general* aesthetic value standing in need of explanation: that the particular aesthetic values we encounter themselves have value? After all, very often such general specifications of the value of all objects of aesthetic appreciation are pretty useless. Either they are too specific to do justice to the range and diversity of art, or else they are too general and vague to be in any way illuminating.

But if the value of objects of aesthetic interest is always something particular then again causal explanation of what is important about aesthetic phenomena is simply impossible. There isn't only one sort of thing to explain.

But just how far the autonomy of aesthetic phenomena extends, to the activity alone or to all the individual objects of aesthetic interest we encounter, the sort of historical explanation posited here must be antipathetic to it.

Quickly drawn, these are the sort of charges levelled against broadly Marxist theories of art and aesthetic activity.

history is essential

Such critics are, unsurprisingly, themselves charged by their Marxist opponents with hubris, restrictive and oppressive politicisation, and with an ironic disregard for the nature of the aesthetic phenomena, upon close attention to which they pretend to place so much stress.

Those who are committed to the essential autonomy of works of art are charged first with trying to lodge culture and class-specific interests into the very fabric of the world, disguised as 'timeless' or 'universal' aesthetic values. Whether conscious or unconscious in intention, deliberate or semi-automatic in its execution, the mechanism of this process of projection has three main components: selective patronage, critical interpretation and the idea of art history. Together these components constitute what can be thought of as an ideology of the aesthetic.

loading the dice

First, those who support the idea of aesthetic autonomy participate in the encouragement of only those traditions and examples of artistic practice which seem best to represent the interests and therefore the values of a particular economic group, the group in power. They then feign wonder when, upon inspection of the prevalent traditions and examples, the same values pop out again. But they are now metamorphosed into apparently culture- and class-independent aesthetic values.

The second mechanism of projection is more subtle. The existence of different cultures in different times and places implicitly suggests the contingency of the *status quo* in our own, and with that, the dangerous possibility of change. Therefore the knowledge we acquire of such cultures through their artefacts must be controlled in such a way as to transform these too into the service of the relevant group. Thus approved methods of interpretation and criticism, assumed to be either objectively scientific or harmlessly individualistic, are used to transform the challenge of the artefacts of other cultures into more comfortable 'archetypes', 'precursors' or 'parallels' of our own. Though, of course, nothing from another culture is allowed to be a 'development' of, or 'departure' from, anything in our own!

Crucial here (this line of criticism continues) is the invention of the idea of art history. This is conceived as a process running parallel to actual history but logically independent of it. It is essentially a proxy for actual history whose most important property is just that respect in which it differs from actual history – its manipulability. This history of art is given a *logic* of development. Phases follow periods as conclusions follow premises. And this supposed logical succession blinds us to the lack of genuine temporal and material succession.

The history of art is thought of as a progress of technical innovation and maturation of insight. But in reality it is only a set of premises for the institutionalised misinterpretation of other cultures and our own past. For, of course, the inevitable line of development always ends *here*. Or, at least, in the last 'artistic movement' that we have 'identified' and for which we have especially designed a new twist in our ideology of the aesthetic.

Aesthetic colonialism is not therefore, like other forms of colonialism, restricted to the exploitation of only those cultures with which we are contemporary. It is possible to reach back into the past to legitimise present practice. Thus the idea of the history of art is nothing but the spurious justification of present political reality thrown backwards over our own shoulders. As only one example of this, note the very well-documented involvement of the CIA in the promotion and export of Abstract Expressionism in the Cold War years as 'The Triumph of American Painting'. MOMA, New York, as the inevitable successor to the Lascaux caves!

In this powerful combination of 'critical' interpretation with historical 'description', the apparent universality of culture and class vision is consolidated by the mutual reinforcement of method and object. It is one thing to 'politicise' works of art by pointing to their essential connection with history. It is something of a different order and truly deserving of the term, to use works of art to politicize the whole of history.

This leads to the third charge. The view that art is autonomous makes only a pretence of attending to the actual phenomena. For a further subtlety in its manipulation is its insistence that the only proper object of attention is the work of art's appearance. This achieves a number of things.

First of all it assimilates works of art to natural objects and thus hides from us the fact that these objects were conceived and produced in particular conditions. This heightens the sense of their universality. In addition, allowing the conditions of production of such objects to appear irrelevant justifies the transformation of artefacts from other cultures into artefacts of our own. We can have access to what is worth having in other cultures without bothering to acquaint ourselves with their realities.

Secondly, the insistence on appearance is a highly effective sanitizer. For should any artefact which challenges current practice, either from our own culture or from that of others, actually survive this onslaught, the relevant properties can be safely put away with what is subjective, personal, a matter of opinion.

So, through this aesthetic of appearance, it is possible to use works of art to objectify current culture and class interests whilst relegating the possibility of change to the subjective and so, by association, to the illusory. That we do not by and large even notice the contradictions here is testimony to the comprehensiveness of the deception.

In all this there is no close attention to the phenomena of art for the sake of works of art. There is only misdirection of attention for the sake of will to power.

These, crudely sketched and at their most forthright, are the main lines of the Marxist attack on 'traditional' or sometimes 'analytic' or 'idealist' aesthetics, criticism and art history.

Unlike the earlier critique, however, the Marxist critique issues in an account of the sorts of difference there are between art and bunk insofar as we consider their relation to tradition and history. In fact, it issues in three different sorts of account, depending upon just where in this tradition of thought people place themselves. Because of their influence both on the recent history of the arts and on current schools of critical thought, it is worth saying a little more about them.

'all art is bunk'

According to what is probably the least sophisticated of the strands of thought in this sort of critique, the ideology of the aesthetic dominates not just our understanding of works of art. It has succeeded in reaching into and transforming whole tracts of our experience. On this view, the 'aesthetic' itself is but another of those concepts with which contingent interests and values are laid up in the cosmic scheme of things. It is not that the aesthetic fails to describe an autonomous region of human experience, isolated from historical determination. It fails to describe any region of experience. That we think there is anything to be salvaged from the concept is simply testament to the power of cultural and class interests to reach into consciousness. We are better off without it.

Quite what is and what isn't true in a situation thus described is difficult to fathom. But it would not be unreasonable to suppose that on this view all 'art' is 'bunk'.

A second strand takes a different view. We need to hang on to our concepts of art and the aesthetic just in order that we can become aware of their historically contingent character. And this means a painstaking and detailed analysis of particular cases of the transformation of such historically determined values into the timeless and the universal. Here art historians, critics and artists all have a role.

what art historians should do
First, those art historians persuaded of this view, should practice a kind of art history whose principal objective is to expose the misreadings to which we have subjected the artefacts of past cultures. The method is one of amassing the evidence which allows the identification of those moments in history when the artefacts actually acquired their supposedly 'timeless' values. Or, where such precision is not possible, of identifying the longer term factors and trends through which the significance of such artefacts in their home culture comes to be painted in our own colours. In this way it is possible to see the extent to which perhaps all our categories, not just those in terms of which we describe such artefacts, reflect not the world but only our history and methods of social and economic organisation.

Such rereadings and reminders are often surprising and enlightening. It is salutary to be reminded, for example, that the form which in the popular imagination constitutes the paradigm of timeless spiritual and physical beauty – the Venus de Milo – would look to its maker and his contemporaries exactly what in fact it is – that of a terribly mutilated woman. Damaged, scarred, no longer holding the tokens that gave it significance. What could it mean to them?

The current debate about whether the British should 'restore' the Elgin Marbles is another useful reminder here. Whatever the rights and wrongs of plunder, it is necessary to remember that the average modern Greek citizen is just as disturbed as the average foreign tourist to discover the 'lurid' colours in which the Parthenon would originally have been decked. The classical does not look like that. It does not feel like that.

But then as this view insists: the classical is not a term which refers to the home culture of such artefacts. It refers only to our own culture via that of others.

what critics should do

On this view critics too have a part to play in enlivening our sense of the contingency of our culture. A principal role of critics should be to sort through the artists who have gained preferment and exposure in our own culture and, by a process of disassembly and then reassembly, seek to disentangle the significance of these works from their critical interpretation inside the ideology of the aesthetic. As a result of this process it may be possible to see one of three things.

First, at some level beneath its surface, the work mirrors the contradictions of the ideology of which it is the product. Perhaps even those contradictions implicit in the idea of the objectivity of appearance.

Or secondly, this truly critical process will reveal that the artist's conformity with the *status quo* of social and/or artistic practice is only apparent. Beneath its innocent surface, the work seeks actively to subvert and expose the artistic and (by implication) the social practices to which it pays lip-service.

Or thirdly, the work may be placed somewhere between these two points, so that it perhaps successfully attacks some aspects of the ideology implicated in its condition of production whilst remaining quite blind to others.

It is no coincidence that such critical strategies are alleged to be particularly fruitful in the critical interpretation of film – a medium whose possibility as an art form, independent in relevant ways from drama, is still not yet apparent to everyone. Because of their very nature, the institutions and hence the conditions of production of film appear open to inspection in a way that seems simply not the case in other, less public, media. And what, according to some at least, we find in such critical inspection and interpretation is precisely this sort of scale of differences. At one extreme, there are works which are of interest because of the way they mirror the tensions in their circumstances of production. These may be films which merely illustrate the moribund values of society. Or which exemplify the somewhat pathetic attempts of the controlling studios to keep control of popular enthusiasm for new developments both within the medium and in the world outside.

But there are also works which, in their subversion of the conventions governing particular genres, for example the 'Western' or the 'Musical', succeed in turning the conditions of their production back upon their owners. They do not merely illustrate but describe and criticise their origins. And there are also works which have a foot in both camps or about which there is substantial critical disagreement as to how they should properly be interpreted.

Something similar is true of the visual arts and indeed all the media of art. It is true that the application of this kind of approach to music proves problematic. But, so far, the application of any critical method to music proves problematic.

what artists should do: two strategies
Last of all, there is a clue here for the practice of contemporary artists. For their task should be to emulate those artists of the past who have become conscious of the ideologies enshrined in their media. Though naturally they need to do this in ways relevant to their own chosen medium and to the changed circumstances of the present.

A principal means to this end is the idea that if the important issues are exemplified in the way the medium itself is conditioned, then there is no distinction to be drawn between works which are socially committed and works which seek to teach us something about the medium in which they are cast. Formal innovation has therefore an important part to play in revealing what must be contingent features of the current concept of art.

According to this view, if it is possible to create an object which is recognisably an object in that medium and yet which does not exhibit certain traditional features, then the features excised must only be accidental features of the medium. Thus, for example, if the idea that works of art ought to be somehow unique, rare or the product of personal endeavour is merely socially relative and is not a necessary feature of art, then it will be interesting or valuable to make works which stress and even proclaim to the exclusion of everything else their non-uniqueness and the lack of technical skill which went into their creation.

It must, however, be admitted that works which seek to raise awareness of the contingency of features of the medium in this way, may bear a superficial resemblance to those works which, in being concerned with the technical innovation of form for aesthethic ends, actually exemplify the very ideology in need of being attacked.

An alternative, more radical, strategy therefore suggests itself. One effective way to avoid this confusion is to present works in the proper context, with all the requisite surroundings of gallery wall or floor, lighting and so on, thus priming the audience to expect what they understand as works of art. They are then presented with objects which are simply not intelligible if understood in the light of the current contingent concept. Indeed, since what matters here is only the exposure of contingency through the mismatch between expectation and object, the artist does not have to present an object which is intelligible in the light of some *other* concept of a work of art. All that matters is the mismatch. That can be guaranteed by producing objects which it can never make any sense to find intelligible. So, if the idea that paintings are something more than simple physical objects is merely an offspring of the ideology of the aesthetic, then this can be shown by producing a 'painting' which is only a physical object and yet which is accepted as a work of art.

two sorts of bunk

And so this second, more sophisticated strand of thought that we have been following does not simply dismiss all art as bunk. Rather, its view of the relation of art to history and tradition allows of two separate accounts of the sort of difference there is between art and bunk.

One account remains laudably straightforward. On the more radical view that artists should serve social ends by shocking audiences into an awareness of the contingency of the notion of art, the difference between art and bunk is that 'art' is not valuable but bunk is. It is just such a thought that took up residence in the doctrines associated with Late Modernist sculpture and painting. Indeed there are very many objects in the traditions of the 'sixties and 'seventies which were the result of a desire to produce deliberately unintelligible objects. That despite the efforts of such artists, many critics, philosophers and audiences continue find everything from objects buried at the bottom of 1 kilometre holes to people sitting in baths of offal aesthetically intelligible (as earlier they did Duchamp's *Fountain*) must be testament to the difficulty of the task to be accomplished.

The point of all this? Only to show that our ways of seeing are indeed our ways of seeing. And not the ways in which things must be seen. Hardly a rationale for a whole medium.

On the less radical account, the difference between art and bunk is ultimately the difference between works which do not and works which do merely reflect the paradoxes of their origins.

On this view, works which merely reflect their origins fail as art because they are incapable of rewarding the sort of interest we normally call aesthetic. Such works are slavish and pedestrian. It is certainly possible that a film may be slavishly conventional and yet still be interesting. For there are lots of other kinds of interest, aside from aesthetic interest. Such a film may be extremely interesting as a kind of biographical or social document. But our relation to works which merely reflect their origins is a relation not to a work of art but to a piece of evidence.

But what now of our interest in the works which are supposed to be art? The problem is that on this view our interest here is also solely directed to what these objects are able to reveal of their origins. It is just that such works display their awareness of their origins. And so, on this view, the sort of difference there is between art and bunk is in the end not an aesthetic difference at all but the sort of difference there is between being a social document and being a social critique. The natural conclusion of this view is therefore that through self-consciousness, art transcends its history.

But if, on this view, works of art can be more than products of historical conditions, we might well wonder just what the difference is between this sort of account and 'Idealist' aesthetics.

The third strand of thought here adds an important new element to this tradition of thought. And this too issues in an account of the sort of distinction there is between art and bunk. What is added to the account are two simple insights. First, that what is a contingent feature of human life and society is not necessarily a transitory feature. Second, that it is a strange kind of emphasis on the physical determinants of human history and culture that includes economics but excludes biology! And so what is added to these accounts, and what transforms them, is the insistence on the overwhelming importance of a background of human biological and psychological structures and capacities (in fact precisely those sorts of deep facts about us with which our last chapter was in part concerned). What difference does this make to the debate?

It makes it possible to insist that it shows a fundamental misunderstanding if we think that we have to choose between the recognition of the essentially historical character of the concept of art and the recognition that the notion of the aesthetic picks out an autonomous area of human experience. For the history which is relevant to the concept of art is the history of a particular kind of being and its experience.

The relevant difference between art and bunk is not that one transcends the limitations of its conditions of production whilst the other is a product of its history. On the contrary, the difference is between works which are products merely of the flotsam of the moment and those which live in an authentic relation to the relatively undisturbed sea-bed of human history, which really are products of the history of this kind of being. A history which includes, as far as we can tell, the paintings of the Lascaux caves. For they too belong to the history of what this being has done with certain materials; the history of a medium.

Having at least acquainted ourselves with the larger battle over the relation between art and history, let us ask a smaller and perhaps more illuminating question: what sorts of difference between art and bunk arise out of considering the relation of works of art not to history in general but to the history of a medium; the traditions of art?

reprise

We have already noticed some relevant factors in our account of the place of intention in art. For as we saw, if an artist fails to produce a work of art she may yet produce something which comes to stand in important relations to other works of art, which is perhaps shown or performed alongside works of art and which becomes part of the history of the medium.

We saw that such an object could be aesthetically interesting in different ways. It might have the sort of interest which anything may have when we are in the grip of an intensified sensitivity to the particularity of things. Or it might have aesthetic interest only under very transient conditions, to a particular sort of person on a particular sort of day. As a certain tree might after the rain. Or it might have a kind of aesthetic interest about which we could agree as a particular boulder or a particular river might. In addition to any of these sorts of interest, it might have a documentary interest as the record or trace of something that was a work of art. All these sorts of object can find useful roles alongside works of art and come to occupy places in the history of a medium.

But when we come to an object of one of these kinds with

a concept of art in our eyes, even with a relevant set of capacities in place, nothing in the work answers to the sort of interest we have in it. It is an object we know to have been made intentionally but there is no intention in the work. Our attitude towards it remains, reluctantly, perhaps sadly, an attitude towards an object.

It is important to note that there is nothing wrong with having such objects alongside works of art. On the contrary, our attitude towards the visual arts, and perhaps the visual arts themselves, would be healthier if we did not keep thinking that all talk about works of art *must* be aesthetic talk about works of art and everything in a gallery, say, *must* be a work of art. Things start going wrong when we try to put everything we say and everything we see in this context inside the concepts of the aesthetic and of a work of art. For we end up distorting the shape of these concepts.

What must be remembered is that, first, if we insist that nothing can fail to be a work of art in these sorts of ways we start to forget the point of succeeding; and second, such objects do not become works of art by being placed next to objects which are; and third, that it is possible for such objects to have a place alongside works of art only against the background of the production of objects which are works of art. Such phenomena are useful comparisons or refreshing on the eye or sorts of overture or coda but only because they exist just inside the borders of a tradition which does not consist only of such objects.

It is just this question, of the way in which an object may be parasitic upon works of art, that brings us to an important sort of difference between art and bunk in their relation to tradition.

an artist with a problem
Imagine an artist who produces a painting which is a solution to a particular sort of formal problem in his medium.

Note, first of all, the idea of a formal problem in a medium. What might this be? What does it involve?

To take a simple and crude case, it might be the problem of

how to suppress the primitive significance of a certain colour in painting or particular shapes in sculpture. We have seen that colour and shapes can acquire such properties in virtue of that part physiological, part psychological, part cultural inter-penetration of property and significance is a necessary back-ground to any concept of art. So the problem might be to somehow tone down or eliminate or perhaps transform the significance with which some physical property has come to be invested because of this background.

For example, the artist might try to make a large block of stone appear to be hollow. Or try to give a large heavy piece of wood a feeling of masslessness.

Some things are clear right away about such problems and their solutions. First, there is no point in solving them, there is no solving of them, if this has already been done in a way that is relevantly reproducible. If such a mass effect has already been achieved, then, if this is a technical problem, there already exists a technical solution. If it is something more than a formal problem, of course, it may be that past solutions are not relevantly reproducible. So if there is a point in solving this formal problem, then this activity already presupposes a tradition which has not yet needed or not yet acquired its solution.

It follows that an artist who makes something that is only the solution of a formal problem that has already been solved has done nothing of any interest. If this is its *sole* property then this is not a work of art. No more than if I now drop two weights out of my study window, am I conducting a scientific experi-ment. It isn't that we do what we do badly. Its just that what we want to do can no longer be done. This is why, as we saw earlier, difference, innovation, originality can be expressions of aesthetic judgements in relation to works of art but, of course, are irrelevant to the enjoyment of natural objects.

But it will also be true that if the way the object looks does constitute the solution to a real formal problem, then it will not be possible to correctly understand this object solely as a physical object. Just on their own, physical objects are simply not the sorts of things that can be solutions to problems. And so if there is something defective in its solution to this problem or something defective in the problem to which it is the solution, what the artist has made cannot, as it were, fall back on its status as an aesthetically interesting physical object. It is too late for it to be seen as that.

There have indeed been many objects produced by artists, especially in the post-war years, which seem to be exhibited solely on the strength of this double-act. Where such objects seem dull or defective as solutions to formal problems, we are asked to see them in terms of their status as aesthetically interesting physical objects. When, considered simply as physical objects, they strike us as dull or commonplace, we are asked to see them as technically innovative works. The result is that we feel confronted by something impossible; a stream of failed physical objects.

medium and material
Something else follows from the idea of a formal problem: how we must think of a medium.

This formal problem, however it might be more precisely specified, *can* be further specified only through an account of the medium and other works in that medium. Thus someone might say that they are trying to avoid just that sort of massiness that they find in so many Henry Moore pieces. And the reason for doing this is perhaps that it is no longer fitting for sculpture to be monumental.

The problem, then, is a problem in the medium. It is not, therefore, a problem solely about wood or stone; a problem which perhaps biologists and geologists might be trying to solve. But this is to say that wood and stone are *not* the media of sculpture. And if that is so, then nor is paint the medium of painting nor human movement the medium of dance, nor language or its sounds the medium of literature and poetry.

This may seem a surprising conclusion. But it is what we believe. If we doubt it, this is only because we are so liable to think that we should attend to the appearance of the object; how the material looks, rather than to the appearance of the work; how the medium looks. We are then tempted to think of an artist's *material* as his medium.

Yet if we reflect, we see that we have the idea of the history of a medium and yet we do not think that it is wood or stone or pigment, or movement or words or celluloid that have the relevant history; that have a tradition. It is the employment of such materials in characteristic sorts of ways which forms the history of the medium. It is just such employment that we understand by the concept of a medium.

It is ironic that we have to remind ourselves of the use of this term when in a different but related context, because the term 'media' is used *ad nauseam* to refer to newspapers, magazines, television, and radio, and not to ink, paper, and electromagnetic radiation.

The poet's task then is not to make his medium, language, deliver up the art, poetry. It is to be so fluent in his material, language, to know how the medium, poetry, can deliver up the art, this poem. The composer's job is not to make his medium, sound, into art, music. It is to make his medium, music, into this work, art. And so the media of art are not, in some cases physical material, in other cases abstract material. They are all sorts of uses of material.

This is not to deny that the nature of the material and how it must be handled plays a determining role in what sorts of things may be produced. There can only be the transmission of ways of using pigment and canvas – even for someone to depart from in interesting ways – if these are indeed ways of handling this material with all its specificities. To insist that the material is only part of the medium is only to point out that the art does not lie in the handling of the material. The art lies in the handling of the medium. The artist's job, before he can make anything, is to master his medium. Which is to say, to master his material together with the ways of handling this material to be found in his culture; though by no means everywhere in his culture and by no means only in his culture.

Nor is this to merely recommend a change in terminology. For to use the term 'medium' to refer to the material alone is to leave ourselves without a term to refer to the handling of the material. And this leads to confusion. It leads for example to the thought that, when painters in the visual arts insist on the *physicality* of their medium, they must either be telling us something blindingly banal – that paint is paint – or else are trying to convey some further semi-mystical insight that can only be expressed in tautologies. In fact, they may be trying to get us to see that the concept of the medium under which they labour, binds them not only to ways of seeing and thinking things, but also to ways of moving, ways of doing things, ways of becoming exhausted.

This also suggests that when artists, as they do in all the arts, speak of the resilience of their medium, its resistance to easy manipulation, that there has to be a struggle, they are thinking as much about the history of the activity in which they are engaged as they are about the physical intractabilities of the material immediately before them.

don't ask for the material; ask for the use
Finally, to insist on the importance of the idea of a medium within which are embedded traditions, rules, maxims, ways of going on, is not to deny that people may work against the grain of tradition and history or may produce art in relative isolation from the traditions of the medium. On the contrary, we need this notion to explain how there can be a grain against which an artist may set himself.

Similarly, there can be so called 'primitive' painters only because a medium is founded on primitives: not the primitive material, but primitive ways of handling the material. This alone does not, of course, constitute an explanation of the true prodigy. But then it is hard to see what would be an explanation here. Such cases are as much a mystery for mathematicians, linguists and chess players as for artists. It is, however, no coincidence that 'primitive' works of art have so much in common. Nor is it a mystery that one of these common properties is just the appearance of tremendous ease with the material. In the absence of demands from the medium, there is not nearly so much to have to master. But then there is much less that one can do. As the fact that such works are always seen as 'primitive' shows us, there is only so much you can do with paint alone.

The history of forgetting that we need this concept of a medium is the history of some of the grosser sorts of bunk both in aesthetics and in the practice of art.

Misplacing the idea of a medium, we say that the media of the arts bear no relation to each other because in some cases we have physical material; in other cases we have human action and movement; in other cases we have sounds; elsewhere words. Now we ask ourselves: 'words are not like colours at all; how can these things have anything to do with each other?' And we abandon the idea of a concept of art before we begin.

Or, worse, we may say that literature has meaning because its medium, words, have meaning. Let us now try to understand the meaning of music in terms of how sounds and collections of sounds are like words. And we are led off in the direction of a 'language' or 'sign system' of music.

Or, worst of all, we may say that paint is the medium of painting so whatever we do with paint is just extending the medium. Which is to extend what painting can mean. And so people start pouring paint down holes or sitting in baths of paint as if this were some kind of insight or liberation. And this works in reverse too. People see, correctly, that the medium of sculpture is not stone or metal or things which may occupy space. And so they think that therefore they don't need to use things which have a relation to space. And so they drink gin or mutilate themselves instead and call themselves sculptors.

This is not to say that the more disastrous of the lunacies that permeated the visual arts in the 'sixties and 'seventies can be put down entirely to such confusions; only that such confusions weaken the constitution and allow whatever more general malaise is at large to gain a tighter grip. One way to avoid this is to keep hold of the notion of a medium. To paraphrase a famous philosophical saying from a not irrelevant context – don't ask for the material; ask for the use.

Reflecting on even this crude formal problem then shows us something of the importance of the idea of a medium as a set of ways for handling a material. A formal problem exists only in relation to a history of uses of the material. And this indeed is what makes it in any way important that a work of art be the solution to this problem. For, amongst other things, it is in relation to this medium that innovation is possible.

appealing to the tradition

Consider our object again. Let's say it is a huge stone block. And the first thing that comes to everyone's mind when they see it is how hollow it seems. We might now ask: what sort of significance can this work of art have?

Clearly it might be interesting or curious or even moving as a physical object. It might be, say, at first rather disconcerting and then peculiarly satisfying to dwell on the incongruity between what we know it to be made of and what we feel it to be like. Or it might simply remain rather eerie – something we would rather not look at. But all this is no different from how a natural, though no doubt very curious, object might seem to us. If this object is the solution to a formal problem then it must be something that it makes sense to look at and think about in a different way from this. We need to know what sort of connection there is between this object's hollow appearance and why it was made this way. What sort of interest or importance there is in the fit between how it looks and why it was made.

And here, if this work is solely the solution to a formal problem, there may be nothing we can do except to appeal to the history of the medium of which the work is part. For we may justly take the work, in exhibiting the hollowness of its material, to be showing us something about the traditions in this medium. It looks the way it does because the artist wanted us to see something about the use of this material in the medium; that this property has always been there in the material but no one has seen it or done anything with it. Or that when we see that this property isn't there in other works we feel differently about them. And now perhaps we go and look at something else and we think, 'Yes now I see – these *do* look somehow just stuffed with themselves'. And this is what happens in the history of a medium. Formal innovation leads to new ways of seeing which leads to new objects of expression which in turn demand more formal innovation. This is not a mysterious process. It is far from peculiar to art, let alone to the visual arts.

The object concerned only with the solution to a formal problem, then, may be intelligible because it points back to new ways of seeing the past or forward to new potentialities in the medium. But, if so, then it is intelligible solely in relation to works which are not concerned only with the solutions to formal problems. It makes sense to ask how its appearance is connected with why it was made, because other works haven't or other works could or other works will make use of the property which it exhibits.

Unless this is true, we shall have to say that the interest of the work lies solely in its physical properties, here the apparent hollowness of a large solid object. But if we are interested only in its physical appearance then, other things being equal, our attention to this work is of a piece with our attention to natural objects that are interesting in this way. And this means that we cannot think of the appearance of this object as the solution to a formal problem in the medium. So, there can be works of art which are intelligible only in terms of formal innovation because there are works which are not intelligible in this way alone.

Clearly, the relationship between a particular work of this kind and a tradition of using the medium will be a matter of degree. Determining this is a matter for art history and criticism. Retrospectively, we may be able to say that such and such a work enabled a new kind of expression, though in itself it expressed nothing but a kind of confidence in the medium. Or we may say that such a work had no relation to a tradition of use of the medium. The problems with which it was concerned ceased to be problems. It was in fact a kind of phlogiston of art history. And so whether by accident or design, whether because of the direction in which an artist moves or because of the direction in which everyone else moves, an object made by an artist can cease to have any relation to a tradition of using the medium in the creation of works of art.

But if a work concerned solely with the exploration of the

formal properties of the medium is part of a process of deliberately severing itself from traditions of using the medium, what must we think? Can such an object still be valued in the ways that works of art are valued? Can it still be found intelligible in the way that we have suggested that works of art must be intelligible?

smart ideas

One thing that might happen is this. We find the object intelligible, as something more than a natural object, because we sense or discover or are told its relation to a relatively specifiable background of thought and ideas in terms of which the object is supposed to make sense. So that to understand the work is to see these ideas come alive in the object. And it is against the background of these relatively specific ideas rather than against a tradition of using the medium that the work is intelligible: 'That's what is on his mind – that's why he wants it to look hollow; now I see how to go on with it!'

Now, of course, the sorts of ideas and intellectual traditions and movements which enter into the practice of the arts are enormously complex. The intellectual background to a medium is as wide as the culture. And this is so complex that there is nothing generally illuminating to say about it. We need here only remind ourselves of its variety.

If we confine ourselves only to the last few decades it is clear that the range in the relatively identifiable sorts of principles, ideas, doctrines, theories and so on that have entered into the visual arts is huge. Such collections of ideas range from the purely formal and painterly through to the overtly political, of all shades of opinion, and anti-opinion, and on to the jokey and the funny and also to the religious and metaphysical.

The point of entry of such contemporary thought into the arts is also various. It may be at the level of the individual artist or through groups of artists or through the manifestos and magazines of self-proclaimed movements. Or such ideas may be explicitly transmitted through the activities of critics and art historians, or tacitly imparted though art educational institutions and through the relations between generations of artists.

Just as varied are the sorts of attitude that some particular artist may have to such ideas. She may regard them as her own property or as the air she breathes, so that she hardly notices them. Such ideas may be more or less assimilated, translated with loss into precepts for artistic practice, sceptically adopted for a trial period and so on.

And in regard to a particular work, artists may simply draw upon such ideas as a means of rubbing along or incorporate them into working practice, or use them defensively and retrospectively in justification of their work.

All this is possible and obvious. How such a more or less identifiable intellectual background is relevant to a particular artist is again a question for criticism, not for philosophy. Clearly, given the variety in the sources, point of entry and character of reception of the intellectual milieu of a culture within a medium, it would be wildly unfair to treat all the ideas belonging to a medium or an artist's conception of that medium at a particular time as if they were theses in a philosophical journal! Otherwise we'd find that we couldn't accept anything about the work because we couldn't accept one of the ideas that lies behind it.

Indeed, we often forget that it is a fact about aesthetic interest that we may find only *something* in a painting or in a novel, or in a piece of music or in a play, dull or stupid or uninteresting. Its style is dated perhaps, or it is mannered or clumsy in some aspect of its execution. We may be unsympathetic to some aspect of a work or find parts of the work, what it wants us to believe perhaps, stupid or morally problematic or ungenerous. And yet we may for all that find something we value, its economy, or its charity, or the way in which it works hard to yoke its elements together. Or indeed its formal innovations. It is a symptom of how we run past the sort of importance that works of art have to think that we cannot value a work for *something* it has or does; only everything; only its 'unity'; to think that because a work of art does not succeed everywhere, it cannot succeed anywhere.

But our concern here is not with works in which there is something else to find. We are considering works where there is no doubt that the object looks as it does *only* because of its essential connection to a set of ideas or principles. The look of the work has sense, for the artist, and for us *only* through its relation to these ideas. Consequently, in the absence of their relation to a tradition in which formal features of the medium are used to do something, our grasp of such works as works is possible *only* via such ideas. Unless you have a grip on those ideas you don't see what's happening at all.

Now we cannot say here that a work of art fails just because knowledge of some relatively identifiable set of ideas is essential to understanding it. For we have said that we cannot in advance determine what will and what won't make a difference to what is seen. It may be that knowing about Mondrian's theosophical beliefs changes everything we see. Maybe not. When we acquaint ourselves with Bosch's iconographic inheritance, everything looks different. But maybe there is only a change of tone. So we ought not to think that because the way a work looks is intelligible only in relation to some set of relatively specifiable ideas, it cannot be a work of art.

But what can be said is this. Where a work stands in a tradition in which the connection between the formal properties of the medium and the use of that medium has been severed, we are forced to seek the intelligibility of the work entirely in the set of background precepts and principles from which it emerges. And if everything about the look of this work is intelligible only in relation to this relatively specifiable set of ideas; if it looks the way it does solely in virtue of its relation to these ideas, principles and precepts, then the whole worth of the work depends upon the worth of these ideas.

And if the ideas and precepts we are left with are bogus, trite or incoherent, then what we are left with is bunk.

flatness

As an example, controversial like any other, consider the emphasis on achieving a perceptually flat picture plane which seemed to be almost a kind of holy grail for so many painters in the post-war period.

We may regard this long-term trait of Modernist and Late

Modernist painting as a symptom of a number of things. Social critics may be right to point to the fact that the pursuit of this formal property in painting is a dramatic symptom of a certain sort of moral surrender; or of a certain kind of numbness in our culture. Or, conversely, of a kind of review and returning. But while these paintings are thought of as symptoms of such things, we cannot use such interpretations to make aesthetic sense of a particular painting now before us. As we saw earlier, this is to treat of the work's natural significance; such talk, important though it is, tries to describe the conditions under which the work was made by seeing how it looks. It is not trying to describe how the work looks, by seeing why it was made that way.

Now it is possible to make sense of the pursuit of this property of 'flatness' in some of these works through their relation to the history of the medium. Thus it is a critical commonplace that the sort of look possessed by the work of some Abstract Expressionist painters may be intelligible because of the relation, through the history of the medium, to the depiction of depth in the picture plane in so-called representational painting. This was a relation mediated by the surrealist use of picture depth to capture the character of the unconscious. In relation to the medium, flatness could be seen not as the pursuit of a physical property for its own sake but as the rejection of illusion and deception. The property of 'flatness' in such works was intelligible as the 'integrity' of the picture plane, parallelling the newfound 'authenticity' of the artist. Whatever we think of such works, if they are intelligible they are so because of their connection with a tradition in which the converse of the property they insist upon has been used to do something. The significance of a 'flat' picture plane is parasitic upon pictures which do not have this property.

But as this tradition developed, this relationship became increasingly tenuous. And, indeed, as this historical relationship weakened so theoretical precepts – a 'principle of flatness' – came increasingly to the fore, conceived by critics and adopted by artists as a kind of credo.

The principle of flatness was adopted by artists as a kind of credo.

According to this doctrine, the reason why it was important to achieve flatness in painting was connected with a view about what painting 'really' was. This had two elements. First the claim that the 'medium' of painting was 'uniquely' and therefore 'essentially' constituted by a two-dimensional surface; that in no other medium do we find such two-dimensionality and every other aspect of painting is found in some other medium. Thus it was claimed by leading and very influential theorists that an enclosing frame was an aspect of the medium of painting also found in theatre. And colour could be found in the theatre as well as in sculpture. And so these aspects of the medium were not unique to and therefore essential to painting.

Of course we might add that colour is also found on the covers of books, and frames are also found holding up sheets of music in orchestras. (Indeed isn't flatness a property of poetry? The page is flat.) It hardly follows that these are relevant or interesting features of the medium. But the plain absurdity of this conflation of medium with material went largely unremarked.

More absurd still was the second half of this claim. This was the idea that since flatness is the only essential property of painting, then painting ought to be concerned with nothing but flatness. The bridge between these ostensibly entirely different, if equally false, claims was this: the thought that, quite generally, the 'Modernist spirit' was one of self-criticism in which areas of competence ought to be as narrowly and therefore as securely drawn as possible. Hence painting should be concerned only with what it was essentially. A flat surface.

What on earth the point of such self-criticism was if not to go on and do something better no one seems to have stopped to think. Failing to see what the point of such a return to 'essentials' might be, being unable to see why anyone should bother, was an inevitable consequence of the confusion of the notion of a material which can have no future and a medium which might have.

And so the visual arts of this period were dominated by the spectacle of works which, bearing no relation to a tradition of the use of the formal properties of the medium, could do nothing but proclaim the existence of their own formal properties; their own non-uniqueness; their own lack of artistic intent. A decade or so later, with the rise of 'Conceptualism', even the objects were left behind; there was only the proclamation. Thus Joseph Kosuth on *Mock Up for the VI Time (Art as idea as idea)*:

> I have changed the form of presentation from the mounted presentation of work in a gallery space to the purchasing of spaces in newspapers and periodicals...This way the immateriality of of the work is stressed and any possible connections to painting are severed...The new work is not connected with a precious object.

It may be objected that it is unfair to try to describe a sort of difference between art and bunk in terms of the coherence or incoherence of the thought that lies behind a work. Isn't after all what counts as incoherent, what counts as bunk, a matter of opinion?

This is wrong. The point is that where the medium has been cast away, these thoughts have to stand on their own. There is no help at hand. They are not to be salvaged by seeing how aesthetically interesting newspapers are. In the absence of the medium which might allow the artist to succeed despite himself, and where what an artist presents to us for consideration has sense only through its relation to such a body of ideas, we must, if we are to be even capable of taking the work seriously, take those ideas seriously. And we can only do this if we believe that such ideas could be interesting and stimulating or could be muddled and incoherent; that they could be illuminating or they could be bunk. And then we have to listen and look and see.

And this in the end is the sort of difference there is between art and bunk in their connection with tradition. In the absence or in the abandonment of the medium, which might yet prove the salvation of a work, what makes for bunk in the arts, what makes for nonsense, sophistry and claptrap, is exactly the same here as it is anywhere else.

fewer than they think

It may be objected that it is a consequence of the views put forward in this chapter, that the many galleries and museums all over the world devoted to recent traditions in the visual arts will not contain the number of works of art they lay claim to. Many will contain a great deal less. Some particularly specialised collections will contain none at all.

But there is nothing perverse in this. No one thinks that any piece of fiction found in a library must be a work of art. No one thinks that anything acted or danced in a theatre must be a work of art. No one thinks this of buildings in cities.

That the thought may be at all surprising is due almost wholly to the confusion of works of arts with aesthetically interesting artefacts and natural objects.

If this view is correct, that we should more carefully distinguish these kinds of object, then one's attitude to approaching such institutions and collections should not be that of wondering to which particular works it would be best to devote one's time. It should be that of wondering if, as well as looking at all the other sorts of interesting objects such collections may contain, one will be fortunate enough to come across any works of art.

notes

p.104. A forceful attack on Marxist conceptions of art history can be found in 'Art History and Aesthetic Judgement' in *The Aesthetic Understanding*, Roger Scruton (London, Methuen & Co. Ltd, 1983) pp. 167-78.

p.106. A useful survey of Marxist theories of art is *Marxism and Art — Essays Classic and Contemporary, Selected and with Historical and Critical Commentary*, Maynard Solomon (New York, Alfred A. Knopf, 1973).

p.108. For an account of the CIA involvement in the export of American Abstract Expressionism see 'Abstract Expressionism, Weapon of the Cold War', Eva Cockburn, *Artforum* XII, June 1974 pp. 39-41. See also *How New York Stole the Idea of Modern Art: Abstract Expressionism, Freedom and the Cold War*, Serge Guilbaut, trans. Arthur Goldhammer (Chicago, University of Chicago Press, 1983).

p.110. The Venus de Milo is discussed by Peter Fuller in 'The Venus and "Internal Objects" ' in *Art and Psychoanalysis* (London, Writers and Readers Publishing Cooperative Ltd, 1980).

p.116. As an example of the change to 'non-reductionist' Marxist thought see 'Art and Biology' *in The Naked Artist — 'Art and Biology' and Other Essays*, Peter Fuller (London, Writers and Readers Publishing Cooperative Ltd, 1983). A useful commentary is *Aesthetics and the Sociology of Art*, Janet Wolff, (London, George Allen & Unwin, 1983).

p.127. The classic work here is Clement Greenberg's essay 'Modernist Painting' in *Art and Literature* no. 4, Spring 1965.

p.130. For Kosuth's work see *Joseph Kosuth — Investigationen uber Kunst & 'Problemkritse' Seit 1965* (Luzern, Kunstmuseum Luzern, 1973).

5: understanding art and understanding people

It is now time to pull together the themes we have been exploring and to restate the main claims of this discussion together with the ideas with which these have been contrasted. In particular we shall say a little more about the sorts of analogy there are between our knowledge of works of art and our knowledge of each other. Between understanding works of art and understanding people.

This discussion began with the question of whether or not a pile of bricks can be a work of art. As we have seen, there are a number of reasons for trying to answer this question.

There is perhaps a clue to one reason for trying to answer it just in the way it is formulated. Can a pile of bricks be a work of art? It may be that it is natural to formulate it in such terms because, as some critics have pointed out, for most people, if Carl Andre's *Equivalent VIII* means anything at all, it is as an especially powerful image of the arts in our culture at a certain time. After all, in its obsessive tidiness, Andre's *Equivalent VIII* is anything but a 'pile' of bricks. It makes sense to call it so because when we have found it unable to be intelligible in its own terms, we have found a way to find it intelligible in our own. For many *Equivalent VIII* has come to be a symbol of the ruins left over from the fragmentation of the concept of art itself: a pile of unintelligible splinters.

In this way, *Equivalent VIII* is regarded as an image *par excellence* of that amalgam of theory and practice, institutions and ideologies, which lasted twenty years and which is known as Late Modernism. Despite the fact that, for the last few years, younger artists reacting against this tradition as well as older artists who have remained relatively isolated from it, are coming to occupy the centre of contemporary artistic practice, the 'stony rubbish' of *Equivalent VIII* remains for very many people the essence of what they understand to be 'modern art'. Curiously, and in this respect, *Equivalent VIII* appears to be standing the test of time.

One reason for attempting to answer the question of whether or not a pile of bricks can be a work of art, then, is that this is also to answer the historical question of whether or not it was possible to produce works of art in a medium, in a certain culture at a certain time. And this is an important question for a medium and for a culture.

A second reason why it is important to ask if a pile of bricks can be a work of art, and the rationale of this discussion, is that this allows us to pose another question which is a useful shorthand for questions about the nature of works of art; what we have, in a deliberately crude way, called the sort of difference there is between art and bunk.

The reason for choosing this way of characterising the relevant sorts of difference should now be apparent. First of all, it does justice to the sort of outrage that characterised the public reaction to Andre's work over a decade ago. And, second and more important, by marking the extremes, the terms of this question go proxy for the whole range of sorts of artistic failure that are possible. 'Bunk' marks the endpoint in the spectrum of the sorts of ways in which it is possible to fail to make a work of art.

And so it has been in the context of species of artistic failure that we have pursued the philosophical question of what sort of thing a work of art is. And this is why we have been interested to see what is at stake in the question of whether or not a pile of bricks can be a work of art.

We should now summarise the main claims of this discussion. At its most general, the claim has been that we can come to understand something of the nature of works of art by correctly understanding the central and classic thought of philosophical aesthetics. This is the thought that, whatever else we must say about aesthetic interest, it is an interest which is directed, in some sense or other, to appearances; that there is a sense in which how things actually are is simply irrelevant to aesthetic interest.

The argument of this book has developed by contrasting two interpretations of this classical thought.

We should first recap the interpretation to which our account has been opposed.

art and appearance

On this interpretation, the relevant appearance of the object of aesthetic interest is always and only how the object seems to me, and is never connected with how the object really is. On this view, the appearance of the object can be detached from the object itself and allowed to take up residence inside my experience, as something I have. And this now seems to be the meaning of the thought that aesthetic interest is, of course, directed through our experience of things.

This interpretation then issues in several further claims.

First, unlike knowledge elsewhere, aesthetic knowledge is conditioned by the nature of its objects. If it is akin to anything, it is akin to knowing that one is having a certain experience; say, having a certain sensation. This is because the relevant sense of how things appear is how they appear to this particular individual now. About this there is only personal knowledge, just as there is about whether or not one is having a certain sensation. And this is a kind of knowledge which either appears as knowledge of the best possible kind, about which someone cannot be wrong, or as something which can never be correct or incorrect and is therefore not knowledge at all.

The second claim on this interpretation is that knowledge of the real origins or history of an object of aesthetic interest is aesthetically irrelevant. This is because the origins of an object are not part of how it appears. But this in turn is because, as the first claim maintains, the object in the world – the *Quercus Marilandica,* or the handle of the knife caught in a shaft of light, or *Equivalent VIII* – is not the real object of my aesthetic interest.

Such objects are only the cause of the real object of aesthetic interest: that experience, which is the appearance, the how-the-object-seems-to-me. And the origins of this object are indeed irrelevant to my interest in it.

The third claim is that since this is so, we can only be interested in those features of an object which are, or which are reducible to, particular perceptible features of the object; of the tree or of the knife or of the arrangement of bricks. We are therefore primarily interested in the physical properties of such objects and the effects of such properties.

The fourth and last claim consists in the application of all this to the phenomenon of art. The thought here is that, despite what may seem to be the case; despite all the surroundings, despite the history, the biographies, the institutions, the markets; despite all that we *can* say about works of art, there is no essential *aesthetic* difference between works of art and all other objects of aesthetic attention.

On this interpretation, then, the only way to take seriously the classic thought that aesthetic interest is centrally concerned with appearance is to deny the aesthetic significance of a distinction between works of art and other sorts of objects of aesthetic interest. Consequently on this view, the triumph of the artist is to succeed in an impossible, because Godlike task: the creation of natural objects.

art and intended appearance

The account offered here rejects this view. Throughout the discussion, the thought has been that we have to take seriously the difference between works of art and other sorts of object.

It must first be admitted that it is not possible to convince someone there is a difference between our aesthetic interest in works of art and our aesthetic interest in other sorts of objects, if they wish consistently to deny this. It has not been suggested that it is self-contradictory to treat works of art as if they were only incidentally made. It is, after all, possible for someone to treat natural objects as if they were made. And so it may be possible for someone to treat all works of art as if they were only natural objects or merely aesthetically interesting artefacts.

But someone who was able to do this consistently would be akin to someone who was capable of treating what others say and do as just the noises and movements made by a kind of automaton. One feels that this would be something more than confining oneself only to the surface of human behaviour. What would be 'human' about this behaviour? Still, however we described it, regarding others in this way would not essentially involve a contradiction. For we should have then to ask upon what set of propositions we found our actual relations with each other. And it is not clear that any set of propositions could play this role.

So the thought at the root of the account developed here is not that the idea of treating works of art as if they were essentially no different from other objects of aesthetic interest involves a contradiction. Only that, if true, it would make a sham of everything which we think about works of art and everything for which we look to works of art.

If we are to understand anything here then we need to be able to reconcile these two thoughts. On the one hand, the true thought that works of art really are different from other sorts of object. And on the other the classic thought – that aesthetic interest is directed towards how things seem rather than to how things are. That there is a sense in which how things really are is simply irrelevant to aesthetic interest.

Unless we are able to do this we cannot understand how looking at a landscape painting and looking at the landscape itself are so different and yet belong together as objects of the same sort of interest. And this means that we will not be able even to begin to understand the relation of our understanding and enjoyment of works of art to the ordinary aesthetic aspects of our lives.

The claims made in the course of the discussion have been generated, then, by the need to understand the classic thought, that aesthetic interest is directed to appearance, given that we need also to take seriously the distinction between works of art and other sorts of object of aesthetic interest.

The principal claims we have been concerned to make are these.

The first claim is that the ordinary trivia of life are for the most part ordinary aesthetic trivia.

It is important to remember this for it reminds us of two things. It reminds us that because so much of the ordinary detail of our lives is conditioned by aesthetic interest, we should not set out thinking that our experience of works of art must be unrelated to what happens anywhere else. It also reminds us that, when we reflect upon the enormous range in the sort of thing in which we take such an interest, we see that whatever it means for aesthetic interest to be directed towards appearance, it cannot mean that we are concerned only with the physical appearance of objects and ensembles of objects. For we are aesthetically interested just as much in whether the anecdote was told in the right way, whether the way he dances goes with the music, and whether this dish fits the occasion, as we are in the tree in the clearing, the knife handle in the shaft of light and the torn wrapper in the street.

Something being 'right', something 'going', something 'fitting' – these concepts are indeed connected with how things seem. They are entirely relative to a point of view. But they apply to far, far more than the appearance of physical objects.

In getting us away from the identification of 'appearance' with 'physical appearance', this claim provided a foundation for a second.

The second claim tries to specify more precisely the thought that there is a difference between works of art and other objects of aesthetic attention.

This means seeing that the fact that works of art are made in particular sorts of ways is not incidental to our interest in them but at its centre. Works of art are not simply artefacts which have been deliberately made in order to provoke aesthetic interest. They are artefacts, the essential interest of which consists in this fact.

waving, not drowning
This leads to the third claim. If we take this difference from other objects seriously, then when we ask what it is, at an absolute minimum, to be interested in something as a work of

art, the answer must be that we are interested in the appearance of the object as made. If this were not the case then we should not need such a concept. We could be content with that of an aesthetically interesting artefact. So, if appearances are the objects of aesthetic interest, then, in the case of works of art, the relevant appearance is the intended appearance.

The fourth claim was that if this is possible, then the concept of art is not descriptive but regulative. It is not a label which we slap onto the object when our interest in it has ended. It is a rule for the regulation of our interest in the object.

This is not to say that the concept of art does not also have content; that it does not specify anything about what is possible in a particular medium. Indeed it does. But we need to distinguish between those elements of the concept of art which are specific to a culture or a time or a medium or even to a particular artist, and those elements which are necessary. And the claim here is that the only element which is necessary is that the object must be such that it makes sense for us to be aesthetically interested in its intended appearance.

The next claim constitutes an attempt to explain what it is to be interested in the intended appearance of a work of art. Works of art are not just aesthetically interesting artefacts: they are aesthetically intelligible artefacts.

This means that it makes sense to ask why a work of art was made to look as it does. And there is here a crucial analogy between our understanding of works of art and our understanding of people. It makes sense to ask this question of a work of art in the way that it makes sense to ask of someone why they are acting like that. The sort of answer we expect is one in terms of reasons; an answer in terms of how things are for the agent. And what having this answer enables us to do is to see what it is that the agent is doing. 'Why are you throwing your arms about?' 'So that he'll see me.' 'Oh, I see – you're *waving*.'

Similarly, the sort of answer we expect to the question of why, for example, a Rothko painting looks as it does is also in terms of reasons. And to appreciate the religious need behind Rothko's work is to see how those paintings look. This is to see what those paintings are. And so the sort of answers we get when we ask this question are not merely of biographical, or psychological, social or historical interest, though they may be one or all of these things. We come to see why it is aesthetically right or fitting, why, aesthetically, it makes sense, that the work of this particular man should look as it does.

The recognition that works of art are essentially intelligible – that why the object was made and what it is like are not logically distinct – leads to a sixth claim important to the account offered here.

It is not possible to specify in advance just what sort of thing we have to know or understand or be able to do or be, in order that we can come to find a work intelligible. As we saw, that works of art are possible at all is relative to a set of capacities with a vast range in their degree of specificity. And different works rely upon different levels and interpenetration of levels of such capacities, skills, inheritances, ways of going on.

The only limit on the relevance of anything in this huge backdrop of competence and belief will be whether or not its use makes a difference to the intelligibility of the work. As we saw, this may mean more or less intelligible. All that is illegitimate in its relation to the work, what the artist can never rely upon, is that which requires us never to see but always to decode; never to hear but always to translate; never to find but always to fantasise.

It was here above all that understanding something of what an artist makes when he makes a work of art is of a piece with understanding something of how an artist may fail to make a work of art; in the crude antithesis of our terminology, of understanding what can happen in between art and bunk.

a relationship, not an event

This enables us to see another aspect of the analogy between understanding works of art and understanding people. That what we can see depends upon what we bring with us does not mean that, therefore, there is no such thing as aesthetic knowledge or that the work is nothing other than the sum of its appearances. A very similar background of competence is required if I am to understand what you say by understanding why you say it to me. Just this sort of judgement is required when we form views of each other; that so and so wouldn't do that; that that's just what she would do; and so on. Nothing here is guaranteed, cast-iron, to be correct. What we say about others and ourselves of course depends upon what we are and what we bring with us. But no one thinks that this means that there is no knowledge of persons. And so reflecting on the sort of knowledge we have of each other prevents us from mis-understanding the character of the sort of knowledge we have of works of art.

What this means is that one's experience of a work of art is rather less like a special sort of event and rather more like a special sort of relationship.

A further claim is that if what unifies and structures the background competence is the concept of art for a medium, at a certain time and in a particular culture, then the concept of a medium is not the concept of a particular material – paint, words, sounds, movement, but is the concept of sorts of uses of that material. Only because of what has happened in the history of painting is it possible for it to make sense that this painting uses the textural possibilities of paint on the canvas. Only against the background of a sculptural tradition of sorts of uses of materials, can it be in any way significant, whether we think it profound or crass, that *Equivalent VIII* is made up of industrial fire-bricks. The rules and maxims, conventions and customs, the great successes and small sorts of failure – all this constitutes what we understand by a medium. If Andre is all at sea, it is in this medium that he flounders.

And that this concept does have a content, that there are things it makes sense to call rules here, does not mean that everything is specified in advance. It does not mean that in the employment of such a concept in the creation of a work of art, an artist is not free. On the contrary, it is the rules embedded in a concept of art which make possible *artistic* freedom as opposed to just doing what one feels like. It is in relation to these rules that it is possible to do something more than produce paintings randomly or by rote.

And again this is no more mysterious than the role of such concepts, such rules, in our relations with each other. I am not necessarily constrained in my relationship with you because there are some things that can count and some things that cannot count as keeping my promise, being grateful and so on.

So only in relation to such a concept does it make sense to talk of the mastery of a medium, of immersion in a medium. And so mastery of a medium is also mastery of the historical and cultural specifics of a concept of art. And struggles in the medium are struggles for the future of the concept of art, perhaps, as in our own time, for whether or not the medium has a future at all.

last thoughts

The last claim we made in our interpretation of the classic thought of philosophical aesthetics is this. To understand the nature of works of art, as one sort of object of aesthetic interest, is to understand something of the nature of a particular kind of being.

If, whatever else we must say about aesthetic interest, we must say that it is an interest which is directed, in some sense or other, to appearances then we must recognise that, at its most general, what sorts of things are possible as appearances for us necessarily depends upon what sort of things we are. And so reflection on the sorts of order in appearance that we are capable of finding and enjoying, the ways in which things really can fit or fail to fit, really can be right or not work at all, shows us what we can rely upon in each other. And, to this extent, reflection on the sorts of aesthetic order we can discover also shows us the sorts of personal, moral and social orders of which we are capable.

It may be that a second thought, which has often featured in the conclusions to discussions in aesthetics but which can only be lightly touched upon here, will now seem to make some sense. For it may be that the classic thought of philosophical aesthetics directs us to the fact that to be able to see or hear or feel what fits, what goes, what makes sense, to be able to sense these things as perceptible features of the world, is to see the particular ways in which we make the world our world. We are able to see that it is through, and not in opposition to, the specifics of our culture and our history that we make for ourselves a world relative to a shared human nature.

If so, perhaps the classic thought of aesthetics, that aesthetic interest is directed to appearances, comes to this.

I say 'No – hear it like this...' and I play the unfamiliar music. And now I make a certain gesture. This time you say 'Yes – I hear it now.' In seeing how my gesture was a reason for hearing the music in that way, in seeing that my gesture was on the inside of the music, perhaps it is indeed that we are mutually appraised of something it makes sense to speak of as the reality of appearances. On this view the triumph of the artist is to succeed in an appallingly difficult, but still human-sized task; the embodiment of life and thought and feeling in objects; the embodiment of the reality of points of view.

It is in this sense that there may be more than just analogies between understanding works of art and understanding people. But this is something of which one is convinced, if at all, not by listening to philosophical arguments but by understanding particular works of art.

less mysterious and more difficult

This book has tried to provide an introduction to the central questions of aesthetics and the philosophy of art and, through reflection upon the sorts of difference there are between art and bunk, it has tried to provide a framework within which to answer these questions. The key elements in this framework have been first, the idea of a regulative concept of art; second, the idea of aesthetic intelligibility; third, the idea that there are important analogies and connections between understanding works of art and understanding other people. If it has been able to suggest at least something of the way in which these thoughts are of a piece, then what is contained here will have met its objective.

This last element in particular has been a guiding thought in the discussion. Indeed, the thought that we best understand what can go right and what can go wrong in art by reflecting more closely on the nature of our relations with each other, is one that, of the ideas current in the philosophy of art, perhaps might do more than most to help secure a future for the arts in our culture. It may help both artists and audiences to see that the phenomenon of art is just as secure but also just as fragile.

Finally, if the impression left by the arguments and suggestions contained in this book is that the activities of making, understanding and enjoying works of art are both less mysterious and more difficult than some in our time have supposed, then this is well.

suggestions for further reading

The following brief guide to further reading in aesthetics and the philosophy of art is heavily biased towards the accessible and the available.

introductory
  Charlton, William, *Aesthetics*   (London, Hutchinson University Library, 1970).
  Pointon, M.,   *History of Art – A Student's Handbook* (London, George Allen and Unwin, 1980).
  Sharpe, R.A., *Contemporary Aesthetics* (Sussex, Harvester Press, 1983).
  Shephard, Anne, *Aesthetics*   (Oxford, Oxford University Press, 1987).

further
Perhaps the best way to move on from introductory works to advanced study in contemporary aesthetics is via one of the many histories or anthologies of aesthetics. Any of the following collections and surveys will provide plenty of opportunities for enjoyable and instructive browsing.
  Beardsley, M., *Aesthetics from Classical Greece to the Present* (New York, Macmillan, 1966).
  Chipp, Herschel, *Theories of Modern Art: A Source Book by Artists and Critics* (Berkeley, University of California Press, 1968).
  Frascina, Francis and Harrison, Charles, eds., *Modern Art and Modernism – A Critical Anthology* (London, Harper and Row, 1982).
  Hospers, J., ed., *Introductory Readings in Aesthetics* (New York, Free Press Macmillan, 1969).
  Margolis, J., ed., *Philosophy Looks at the Arts* (Temple, Temple University Press, 1978).
  Osborne, Harold, ed., *Aesthetics* (Oxford, Oxford University Press, 1972).
  Royal Institute of Philosophy Lectures Vol. VI, *Philosophy and the Arts* (London, Macmillan, 1973).
  Soloman, Maynard, *Marxism and Art – Essays Classic and*

Contemporary Selected and with Historical and Critical Commentary (New York, Alfred A. Knopf, 1973).

Tillman, Frank A. and Cahn, Steven M., eds., *Philosophy of Art and Aesthetics – From Plato to Wittgenstein* (London, Harper and Row, 1969).

advanced

Cavell, Stanley, *Must We Mean What We Say?* (Cambridge, Cambridge University Press, 1976), Essays III, VII & VIII.

Collingwood, R.G., *The Principles of Art* (Oxford, Oxford University Press, 1958).

Fischer, Ernst, tr. Bostock, Anna, *The Necessity of Art – A Marxist Approach* (Harmondsworth, Penguin, 1963).

Fuller, Peter, *The Naked Artist – 'Art and Biology' and Other Essays* (London, Writers and Radicals Publishing Cooperative Ltd., 1983).

Gombrich, G.H., *Meditations on a Hobby Horse and Other Essays on the Theory of Art* (London, Phaidon, 1963).

Hawkes, Terence, *Structuralism and Semiotics* (London, Methuen, 1977).

Kant, Immanuel, tr. Meredith, James Creed, *The Critique of Judgement* (Oxford, Oxford University Press, 1952) First Part: *Critique of Aesthetic Judgement*.

Margolis, Joseph, *Art and Philosophy* (Sussex, Harvester Press, 1980).

Savile, Anthony, *The Test of Time* (Oxford, Oxford University Press, 1982).

Scruton, Roger, *The Aesthetic Understanding* (London, Methuen, 1983).

Scruton, Roger, *Art and Imagination* (London, Methuen, 1974).

Wolff, Janet, *Aesthetics and the Sociology of Art* (London, George Allen & Unwin, 1983).

Wollheim, Richard, *Art and its Objects* (Harmondsworth, Penguin, 1970).

Perhaps the most accessible guide to the visual arts of the '80s is *State of the Art*, Sandy Nairne (London, Chatto and Windus, 1987). For current and future developments consult *Modern Painters – a Quarterly Journal of the Fine Arts*, edited by Peter Fuller.